GLAM ROCK

DANDIES IN THE UNDERWORLD

ALWYN W. TURNER

V&A PUBLISHING

First published by V&A Publishing, 2013
Victoria and Albert Museum
South Kensington
London SW7 2RL
www.vandapublishing.com

Distributed in North America by Harry N. Abrams Inc., New York
© The Board of Trustees of the Victoria and Albert Museum, 2013

The moral right of the author has been asserted.

ISBN 978 1 85177 764 8

Library of Congress Control Number 2013935518

10 9 8 7 6 5 4 3 2 1
2015 2014 2013

Designer: Will Webb
Copy-editor: Rachel Malig
Index: Hilary Bird

New photography by Jaron James, V&A Photographic Studio

Printed in Hong Kong

V&A Publishing

Supporting the world's leading
museum of art and design,
the Victoria and Albert
Museum, London

CONTENTS

INTRODUCTION
FAR BEYOND THE PALE HORIZON

INTRODUCTION

Bowie is the understudy who's been waiting in the wings for years. Finally his big day comes and he's got every step, every note, every voice-warble right. A star is born.

Gay News

Platform boot worn by Elton John, *c.*1973.
V&A: S.233A-1977.

Even by the standards of its predecessors, the sleeve of Roxy Music's fourth album, *Country Life*, was an arresting image. Against a backdrop of evergreen shrubbery, a flashbulb caught two German models, Constanze Karoli and Eveline Grunwald, looking directly at the camera, clad only in see-through underwear, as they made a token attempt to cover themselves. The record was named after the upmarket British magazine – in a self-deprecating joke about how the group's singer, Bryan Ferry, was being portrayed in the music press as a rock aristocrat – but the picture suggested something entirely different.

In later years, the sleeve would have attracted accusations of sexism, but in 1974 the complaints came from moralists, suggesting that it veered too close to pornography, and in America it was replaced for several years by a cover that removed the women and left only the foliage. Even with that censorship, the resultant publicity was sufficient to help the album become the band's first American hit. 'While I'm pleased with the controversy, I don't think the picture's depraved,' observed Ferry. 'A bit seedy perhaps, but you see far worse things than that.'[1] The group's publicist, Simon Puxley, suggested a little mischievously that the image was 'definitely a contribution to Aesthetic Rearmament'.[2]

The teasing allusion to the Moral Rearmament movement was clearly intended to be tongue-in-cheek, but there was an element of truth to the comment, for the early 1970s did see a new aesthetic being forged in rock music. Acts like Roxy Music, David Bowie, T. Rex and Cockney Rebel in Britain, in

alliance with Alice Cooper, Lou Reed, the New York Dolls and Jobriath in America, created a movement that was by the end of 1972 being referred to as glam rock. It represented a marked turn away from the recent past, and established a style and an attitude that has continued to inform popular music in the decades since.

Its commercial peak was only brief – perhaps the two-and-a-half years from David Bowie's television appearance singing 'Starman' in June 1972 through to Mott the Hoople's valedictory swansong 'Saturday Gigs' in December 1974 – but within that time glam defined an era. What defined glam, however, was slightly less clear.

To start with, there were few who were prepared to associate themselves with the genre. 'I don't think really we were a glam band,' reflected Dave Hill, guitarist with Slade,[3] while Michael Bruce, his counterpart in the Alice Cooper band, shared that view: 'We never really thought of ourselves as being a glam band.'[4] Or, as Dale Griffin of Mott the Hoople put it: 'Glam rock wasn't us.'[5] The liberating effects of the music opened up possibilities for other acts who ventured beyond the existing confines of rock music, but here too there was a disavowal. 'It was easy to see why we got lumped in with the others,' said Georg Kajanus of Sailor, 'but the fact that we were considered part of the glam rock stable was simply a misdiagnosis of my music and our presentation.'[6]

At the pop end of the market, there was a similar reluctance to be associated with what was seen as a media-generated label. 'We were a heavy metal band,' insisted Andy Scott of the Sweet,[7] while Suzi Quatro was more forthright still: 'I didn't wear any make-up and I had a plain black leather suit on,' she pointed out. 'I was the anti-glam. The records weren't glam either, they just happened to be in that era.'[8]

The idea that such pop acts might be considered part of the movement was sufficient to scare off even those who had once aligned themselves with the cause. 'All those glitter groups sprang up and debased the look,' grumbled Bryan Ferry, as he hung up his sparkling tiger-print outfit and slipped into a white tuxedo.[9] Nor was David Bowie much impressed. 'I think glam rock's a lovely way to categorize me,' he had proudly proclaimed in 1972,[10] but his enthusiasm didn't last, and twenty years later he explained his eagerness to dissociate himself from the movement: 'We were very miffed that people who'd obviously never seen *Metropolis* and had never heard of Christopher Isherwood were actually becoming glam rockers.'[11]

If the protestations were to be believed, there was no such thing as glam; it was the rock that dared not speak its name. But the fans knew better, recognizing the clarion call in the Sweet's single 'Teenage Rampage': 'There's something in the air of which we all will be aware.'[12] Even if the boundaries were uncertain and porous, there was a recognizable spirit of the age, common threads running through the acts and a

The man born Bernard Jewry encapsulated glam's interest in reinvention, enjoying two pop careers: first as Shane Fenton in the early 1960s (left), then as Alvin Stardust a decade later (right). Photographs by Harry Hammond (V&A: S.1110–2009) and Harry Goodwin.

Glam fans in London, 1972.

shared agenda. In what was becoming a staid and stodgy rock scene, glam replaced authenticity with artifice, careful craftsmanship with carefree playfulness, and dressing down with dressing up. Theatricality, camp and experimentation were pushed to their limits and won over a mass audience. Seldom had the avant-garde been so accessible.

Those cultural references cited by Bowie, for example, suggest one of the key features of glam: the fact that it drew on, and spilled out into, literature, fashion, design and art. Glam was an inveterate namedropper, revelling in its love of both high and low culture. In the space of a single song, 'Do the Strand', Roxy Music managed to slip in references to the *Mona Lisa*, *Lolita* and *Guernica*, as well as to the Moulin Rouge dancer La Goulue, to the fashionable 1930s restaurant Quaglino's, and to the mashed potato, an early-1960s dance derived from the twist. Hooked by the music, fans found themselves drawn into an account of cultural history

populated by everyone from Beau Brummell to Busby Berkeley, Jean Genet to George Orwell, Kabuki theatre to cult movies. This was rock and roll not merely as entertainment, but as education, the first rock movement to come with a reading list. Frequently pretentious, and sometimes just plain absurd, glam was never boring and always seductive in its pursuit of beauty.

There was an emphasis on staging and style, reflected in the fact that it took longer to design the sleeve to the first Roxy Music album than it did to record the songs themselves. 'We believe in the visuals as much as the music,' explained Alex Harvey,[13] whose group, the Sensational Alex Harvey Band, was amongst the most theatrical outfits in an age of rock theatre. 'We couldn't go onto stage without some form of presentation,' agreed Ferry; 'it makes it more formal. We don't associate sincerity in music with drabness in appearance.'[14] Or, as Cockney Rebel's Steve Harley put it:

'You've no right to be on stage if you don't look like a million dollars, not if you think you're in show business.'[15]

It was an attitude that applied to the audience as well. 'Everybody's in showbiz,' sang the Kinks on their single 'Celluloid Heroes', 'and everybody's a star.'[16] Since the entire process was knowingly artificial, fans were encouraged to play at being stars by artists who were happy to acknowledge that they were doing just the same. 'Up until that time, the attitude was "what you see is what you get",' said Bowie. 'It seemed interesting to try something different, like a musical where the artist onstage plays a part.'[17] Characters were created, roles were tried out in a public arena. The term 'glam' derived, of course, from glamour, and it retained some of that word's original meaning of a magical spell or enchantment, suggesting a transformative moment of escape from reality. Though it was sometimes the case that artistic intent

coincided with the interests of expediency. 'I realized,' admitted Richard 'Kid' Strange, singer with the Doctors of Madness, 'I would have to compensate for my musical shortcomings with sheer force of personality and an element of visual spectacle and drama.'[18]

'Hollywood razzamatazz has come to the world of beat,' marvelled the BBC news programme *Nationwide*, in May 1973, even as it worried about 'what the beat age will spawn next when someone like David Bowie isn't even freakish enough to shock us anymore.'[19] And there was a shock value in glam, a confrontation with conformity through the use of flamboyant costumes and cosmetics that delighted teenage fans precisely

because it annoyed an older generation. 'You've got your mother in a whirl,' teased Bowie; 'she's not sure if you're a boy or a girl.'[20] The playing with sexuality was deliberately provocative. When, in 1973, the television comedy show *The Goodies* made an episode titled 'Superstar' that ridiculed modern music, Bill Oddie was cast as 'a pop star in the David Bowie–Alice Cooper vein', purveying what was referred to as 'poof rock'.[21] That proved too strong for the BBC and the phrase was edited out of the final version, but the perception was far from uncommon.

The self-proclaimed bisexuality of British glam, following on from Bowie, may not have stood up to rigorous investigation, but it made a serious impact on a country where male homosexuality had only been legal since 1967, and then only in very restricted circumstances and not at all in Scotland or Northern Ireland. There was less ambiguity in American glam, where a teenage Lou Reed had been subjected to electroconvulsive therapy 'to discourage homosexual feelings',[22] and where Sylvester, Wayne County, Jobriath and T. Roth (of Another Pretty Face) were entirely open about their sexuality.

Less obviously, many of the artists had in common their long years of underachievement in music. 'We've all spent years working to get where we are,' explained Marc Bolan of T. Rex,[23] after his fifth album, *Electric Warrior*, finally brought him the success he craved. Bowie's first hit was 'Space Oddity' in 1969, his tenth single, but even that didn't herald a breakthrough and for a while he looked as though he were destined to be a one-hit wonder, until sustained success came with the release of his fifth album, *The Rise and Fall of Ziggy Stardust and the Spiders from Mars*. Similarly, Mott the Hoople made the big time with their fifth album, *All the Young Dudes*, and Lou Reed had his only hit with 'Walk on the Wild Side', from his second solo release, *Transformer*, following four albums with the Velvet Underground. Gary Glitter and Alvin Stardust released their first singles in 1960 and 1961 respectively; David Essex, Slade and the Sweet in 1965, 1966 and 1968; and although Roy Wood had enjoyed hits with the Move and the Electric Light Orchestra before forming his own glam band, Wizzard, his track record started with his days 'as both lead guitarist and bewigged Dusty Springfield impersonator in Mike Sheridan and the Nightriders'.[24] Alex Harvey went back yet further, to the dawn of rock and roll itself, when he was named Scotland's answer to Tommy Steele in a 1956 competition.

These were artists who had served long apprenticeships and were now ready for their close-ups. 'Bowie is the understudy who's been waiting in the wings for years,' wrote *Gay News* in 1972. 'Finally his big day comes and he's got every step, every note, every voice-warble right. A star is born.'[25]

Glam stars also shared a fondness for the seven-inch single as an art form, at a time when the format was looking like an endangered species. As the 1970s dawned, singles sales were at a lower level than they had been before the advent of rock and roll, *Top of the Pops* had dropped out of the top twenty charts of television shows, and the album was considered the only respectable medium for rock. 'I don't think we will make any more singles,' sniffed Ian Anderson,[26] singer and flautist with the progressive rock band Jethro Tull, in 1970, and although his group did occasionally break that resolve, many of the most critically acclaimed acts of the time – including Led Zeppelin and Pink Floyd – refused to sully their hands with such ephemera, at least in Britain. Only little kids bought singles, it was believed; such things were inherently trivial, OK for manufactured pop groups and for soul singers, but beneath the dignity of white rock musicians.

Similarly, appearing on *Top of the Pops* constituted an act of selling out to commercialism, compared to the newly launched BBC Two show, *The Old Grey Whistle Test*, which took its music much more seriously and only featured acts who had released an album. Martin Newell, of the Colchester glam band Plod, understood the issue clearly. 'We were concerned with selling out,' he wrote in his autobiography; 'we wanted to do it. How much better, we thought, to be on *Top of the Pops* than *The Old Grey Whistle Test*.'[27] Plod never made it that far, but the advent of Bolan, Bowie and Slade ensured that by 1975 singles sales had recaptured the peaks achieved at the height of Beatlemania, and that *Top of the Pops* was bigger than ever. Glam reinstated the three-minute pop single as the centrepiece of rock and roll. 'If you can't say it in a three-minute song, you can't say it at all,' reckoned Noddy Holder, the singer with Slade.[28]

In the process, glam also returned pop music itself to the heart of teenage culture. The division between albums and singles had raised the possibility that rock might follow the precedent of jazz, and split into mutually exclusive strands of elitist abstraction and middle-of-the-road mediocrity. As the target age of rock fans drifted upwards, there was no inherent reason to assume that rock and roll would attract a third generation; indeed the decline in singles sales suggested that the half-hearted leftovers in the top twenty were insufficient to engage the attention of a younger audience, that other attractions were looming ever larger.

Glam reversed that trend, culturally as well as commercially. In the eighteen months to the end of 1972, as it took over the charts, the three main football magazines in Britain – *Goal*, *Football Monthly* and *Shoot* – saw their combined circulations fall by nearly quarter of a million, while the equivalent music papers – the *New Musical Express*, *Melody Maker* and *Disc* – increased by 120,000. There was a parallel situation in the publications aimed at teenage girls: those with a romantic focus – *Mirabelle*, *Valentine* – were eclipsed by those that pushed music to the fore: *Fab 208* and *Jackie*.

So big did glam become that it lured in existing stars. Rod Stewart and the Faces, who were never part of the genre,

dressed up a bit, put on a show and were included in contemporary newspaper accounts of the phenomenon. The singer-songwriter Elton John began to specialize in over-the-top stage outfits and released the glam-flavoured singles 'Crocodile Rock' and 'Saturday Night's Alright for Fighting'. And the Rolling Stones reclaimed their glam credentials with 'It's Only Rock 'n Roll (But I Like It)', a single that came with perhaps the campest promotional video of the decade, as the band, dressed in sailor suits, were gradually submerged in a rising tide of bubbles.

Beneath all these external expressions of glam lay a crucial shift in an understanding of the nature of rock music, a specifically British take on the music.

When rock and roll was born in 1950s America, it was clearly a derivation of existing rhythm and blues, an extension of the music made by the likes of Louis Jordan, Wynonie Harris or Arthur 'Big Boy' Crudup, blended with country singers Hank Williams and Bill Monroe and with gospel music, all of it repackaged for a younger, more affluent and primarily white audience. In America, therefore, while the early records of Bill Haley and Elvis Presley may have been startling, there was at least a continuity from existing traditions.

In Britain, however, where neither rhythm and blues nor country were part of the existing musical vocabulary, rock and roll arrived fully formed, with no obvious antecedents or roots. The biggest-selling artist in Britain that year was the bandleader Victor Silvester, his strict-tempo music for ballroom dancing having remained largely unchanged for two decades, unaffected by more recent American developments. Meanwhile country and western, insofar as it was recognized at all, was mostly taken to refer to the singing cowboys of Hollywood, of interest only to children. The biggest of those stars was Gene Autry, who came over to Britain in 1953 for a show that ran for four weeks at Earls Court; it revolved around cowboys and Indians, featured an appearance by Champion the Wonder Horse, and was, in Autry's words, 'a show just for us kids'.[29]

Despite these unpromising conditions, rock and roll had a transforming impact on Britain's young teenagers. This was a generation who had spent their childhood in the austerity years – many remembered the happy day in February 1953 when sweets had finally come off the ration – and their adolescence in a country where telephones were far from common, where thousands died from the effects of smog, and where the only television channel (for the minority who possessed a set) ceased broadcasting between 6pm and 7pm to allow parents to put young children to bed. The eruption of rock and roll in 1955 – the same year that brought Britain a second television channel, the first Wimpey bars, Mary Quant's boutique Bazaar and the James Dean movie *Rebel Without a Cause* – swept the nation's youth. It offered an irresistible vision of America, the promised land across the ocean where teenagers were a consumerist force to be reckoned with, and where everything was possible.

As that generation commenced the British annexation of rock in the 1960s, however, there were many who began to scorn the commercial sounds of their youth and to chase after the exclusivity of the earlier music. There was a model here in the post-war jazz revivalist movement that had seen British musicians and enthusiasts become obsessive curators of an American tradition. That pattern was replicated and, by the end of the 1960s, the blues had taken over from jazz as the music of choice for earnest young Britons from the white suburbs who were embarrassed by the banality of their background and who, in search of authenticity, found it in a black American past. 'The blues heroes – John Mayall, Eric Clapton, Fleetwood Mac, Chicken Shack – were bearded, hairy, dishevelled, weary and meticulously grubby,' noted the critic George Melly, as he examined publicity shots of contemporary British acts in 1968. 'The two groups were actually photographed outside a West Kensington slum doorway with an overflowing dustbin. The intention, the image, was of urban poverty, a deliberate rejection of anything smacking of prosperity or compromise.'[30]

In musical terms, glam was, above all else, a reaction to the dead end of this blues-rock, a rejection of its purism, puritanism and veneration of individual musicianship, as expressed through long jam sessions. 'You've heard enough of the blues and stuff,' sang Roxy Music,[31] articulating an archetypal glam sensibility. 'Jamming bores the arse off me,' confessed Mott the Hoople's Ian Hunter,[32] while Slade didn't have any time for such self-indulgence either: 'We took the long guitar solos and threw them out the window.'[33]

The contrast was not merely with a denimocracy that required blues rockers to dress like their audiences and eschew showmanship; it was also about precision and discipline in the music. When Brian Eno joined the nascent Roxy Music, he found that there were no gigs planned, no slog round a circuit of pubs and clubs to acquire an audience, but rather a process of endless polishing: 'There was a long,

long period of just rehearsing these things and going over and over them.'[34] Glam had little time for the pseudo-spontaneity of improvisation, extolling instead the virtues of practice-driven perfectionism. 'All the stuff was worked out, right down to where each individual would stand for the beginning of the number,' remembered drummer Mick 'Woody' Woodmansey, of David Bowie's second American tour in 1973. 'It was like a theatre company.'[35] When Bowie turned to acting, the same approach was evident. 'He would stir the drink with the barrel of the gun,' recounted Paul Meyersberg, who wrote the movie *The Man Who Fell to Earth*; 'third take, he would still stir it exactly the same way, it would be exactly the same movement. Everything matched. It was like he was an automaton.'[36]

If there was a lack of reverence for the roots of the music, however, glam was nonetheless enthralled by 1950s rock and roll. Its stars had also been children when rock first hit Britain, albeit a significant couple of years younger than the future blues-rockers. Recognizing the reality that Britain had experienced rock and roll at one stage removed – that the surface glitz of the music had meant more than its obscure origins in the Mississippi Delta, the Grand Ole Opry or the evangelical churches of the Deep South – glam was happy to revel in the artificiality of that experience, championing what was seen by some as a suspect superficiality.

At its most basic, this was seen in the use of stage names. In the early days of British rock and roll, renaming stars had been standard, with the likes of Tommy Steele, Billy Fury and Vince Eager, but by the 1960s such behaviour had become unfashionable, save for a rare exception like Ringo Starr. Glam revived the practice, so that David Bowie, Marc Bolan, Gary Glitter and Alvin Stardust all operated under pseudonyms. Bill Fifield was renamed Bill Legend on joining T. Rex, while guitarist Luther Grosvenor – already blessed with an impressive name – was persuaded, when he joined Mott the Hoople, to adopt the identity of Ariel Bender.

The return of overtly made-up names came with a nod to the showbiz origins of British rock. 'We were showbusiness,' said Dave Hill of Slade; 'I've always been like that.'[37] In their childhood, the future stars of glam had seen rock and roll fighting for a place amidst the family-orientated light entertainment that dominated the output of both the BBC and ITV. That culture continued into the 1970s, and while the Beatles and the Rolling Stones had rebelled against it, glam seemed happy to play along, so that both Marc Bolan and

Bryan Ferry made appearances on Cilla Black's television variety show, singing duets with the hostess on 'Life Is a Gas' and 'It's My Party' respectively. Ferry also joined Twiggy on her show, the two of them dressed in school uniforms for a take on 'Wonderful World'. Even that implausible performance, however, was eclipsed by the sight of David Bowie singing 'Little Drummer Boy' with Bing Crosby on a Christmas special in 1977.

The fascination with the mythology of American popular culture remained, but there was no pretence that it was anything other than a fantasy. Again there was an honesty about how rock and roll was felt in Britain. 'From England, America merely symbolizes something,' commented Bowie on his first trip to the US in 1971; 'it doesn't actually exist.'[38]

Apart from the music, the initial appeal of rock had lain partly in the fact that the world depicted in its lyrics was so alien and unknowable. Chuck Berry sang about a Cadillac Coupe de Ville, and even the rhythm of the words, let alone the image they conjured up, was unbelievably exotic in a country where the Morris Minor Traveller was a more common mode of transport. Consequently, the use of car imagery in the songs of T. Rex ('You've got a hubcap diamond star halo'[39]) and David Bowie ('Chev brakes are snarling'[40]) owed more to Detroit than to Longbridge, as did Roxy Music's reference to a Studebaker in 'Virginia Plain' and Mott the Hoople's self-explanatory song 'I'm a Cadillac'.

Echoes of the first generation of rock and roll were there both at the birth of glam – the B-side to T. Rex's 'Ride a White Swan' was a version of Eddie Cochran's 'Summertime Blues' – and at its death: the last song David Bowie played before announcing the retirement of Ziggy Stardust was Chuck Berry's 'Round and Round'. The phrase itself was flaunted in a way that was alien to the ethos of the blues revivalists, making an appearance in dozens of song titles, from Bowie's 'Rock 'n' Roll Suicide' through Gary Glitter's 'Rock and Roll' to Wizzard's 'Rock 'n' Roll Winter'. A host of cover versions by glam acts extended even to some critically reviled music: the Sensational Alex Harvey Band attacked 'Giddy Up a Ding Dong' with a manic glee undreamt of by Freddie Bell and the Bell Boys; Bryan Ferry revived the Paris Sisters' 'I Love How You Love Me'; and Eno's one attempt to undertake a promotional tour saw him encoring with Neil Sedaka's 'I Go Ape', as unhip a song as could be imagined in 1974.

Eno also borrowed the phrase 'See you later, alligator'[41] from Bill Haley and His Comets in one of the songs on his debut album, and that element of quotation was another feature of the genre. At the end of T. Rex's 'Get It On', Bolan threw in the line 'Meanwhile, I'm still thinking' from Chuck Berry's 'Little Queenie', a song also referenced in Gary Glitter's 'Rock and Roll (Part One)', alongside 'Blue Suede Shoes' and 'U.S. Male'. Bowie's multiple borrowings included, most happily, 'Look at those cavemen go', from the Hollywood Argyles' 'Alley Oop', which was inserted into the chorus of 'Life on Mars'.

The effect of glam's recycling of existing imagery was to claim rock and roll – now nearly twenty years old – as being itself a tradition, to suggest that its power as a cultural force did not depend on its roots, that it was separate from the sum of its parts. But there was a further implication – that the cultural pre-history of rock and roll was not to be seen in terms of blues and country, but of what was actually experienced from the perspective of a British child. The anguished figure of American crooner Johnny Ray, who had caused near-riots at the London Palladium in the early 1950s, for example, was more significant than an unknown blues singer like Robert Johnson. Similarly, by seeing Elvis Presley as primarily a star, rather than as a country-blues musician, he could be placed in a Hollywood lineage that stretched back from Marilyn Monroe and James Dean through Humphrey Bogart and Marlene Dietrich to Rudolph Valentino.

Others, impatient for a fin de siècle of their own, went back still further, to the dandies of the nineteenth century. 'Oscar Wilde with a slide guitar', was Michael Des Barres's description of what he aspired to with his group, Silverhead.[42] Meanwhile, Carlo Maria Franzero's 1958 biography of Beau Brummell was the favourite book of a young Marc Bolan: 'that's where he started getting the idea of cravats,' remembered his brother, Harry Feld, 'that's where he got the cloaks from in the early Tyrannosaurus Rex days.'[43] Glam tapped into a long British tradition of amused detachment, fleeing from seriousness as well as from hard times, and finding that, in the words of Oscar Wilde: 'To be natural is such a very difficult pose to keep up.'

Susan Sontag quoted that aphorism of Wilde's in her celebrated 1964 essay 'Notes on "Camp"', and there was, of course, a strong vein of camp running through glam. It was hard not to spot it when, say, the Sweet dressed up as what were then called Red Indians for their *Top of the Pops* appearance to promote 'Wig Wam Bam', a pumped-up parody of Longfellow's 'The Song of Hiawatha'. But, for a

**Costume worn by Brian Eno while he
was in Roxy Music, *c.*1972.**
Designed by Carol McNicoll. V&A: S.156–1977.

while at least, low camp co-existed with high culture; at a Roxy Music concert Bryan Ferry might introduce a song as being 'for all you sailors',[44] but it turned out to be 'Sea Breezes', a piece which juxtaposed passages of plangent crooning with a strident middle-section evoking the 1930s music of Bertolt Brecht and Kurt Weill.

There was another strand too, determined to keep its platform boots rooted in reality. 'I think people are getting the same sort of excitement from our act as they do from soccer,' observed Noddy Holder.[45] At its great moments, British rock has always relied on a cross-class alliance between the art school and the assembly line, and glam was no exception. It drew on older cultural strands of the British working class, even in the context of a rock and roll gig. When girls began throwing their underwear on stage at Slade gigs, Holder referred to such items of clothing not as 'knickers', let alone as 'panties', but as 'drawers', and in that choice of language he placed the band firmly within the cheerfully vulgar tradition of the music hall, a world populated by seaside landladies and commercial travellers, saucy young men and sexually frustrated women. The group's 1974 album track 'Find Yourself a Rainbow' was a charmingly old-fashioned song, sufficiently authentic to warrant a cover version by Max Bygraves.

Music hall as a living culture was long gone by the early 1970s, unable to survive the challenge from television, but it remained a powerful folk memory. In an interview at the end of 1969, David Bowie listed his heroes and, amongst the more obvious names of John Lennon and Bob Dylan, he included several veterans of the halls: George Formby, Gracie Fields, Nat Jackley, Albert Modley.[46] Such figures were to be found alongside rock and roll on radio and television in the 1950s (all but Formby were still working at the time of the interview), and glam recognized a kindred spirit. 'Bryan and I always joked about the fact that rock and roll was basically music hall,' remembered Andy Mackay, reeds player with Roxy Music.[47]

Perhaps the biggest star of the halls when the glam artists were growing up was comedian Max Miller, and it's hard not to see him as a precursor to the performers of the early 1970s. Wearing silk suits with enormous plus-fours and outrageously extravagant patterns – a print of white daisies on a blue background was a favourite – set off with pale make-up, two-tone shoes and a white Trilby perched at a jaunty angle, there was a sexual ambiguity to Miller. His catchphrases suggested vanity ('Haven't I got a nice figure, lady?'[48]), arrogance ('There'll never be another') and even gay effeminacy ('So what if I am?'), but his material and his reputation spoke of a rampantly promiscuous heterosexual reality. The softness of his appearance and the way in which he spoke of himself in the third person ('He's a boy, isn't he? I hope so!') were calculated to appeal to women as much as to men, presenting a fantasy figure a long way removed from the hardships of working-class life in the 1930s and '40s. Noddy Holder's stage outfits – particularly his loud tartan ensembles – were said to have been inspired by Miller.

The magician Aleister Crowley was regularly cited by rock musicians: his image appears on album sleeves by the Beatles and the Doors, and he is namedropped by David Bowie in the song 'Quicksand'.

Max Miller was the last great star of the British music halls; his tartan suit was said to have influenced Noddy Holder's choice of stage-wear.

Even more pertinent was another comedian, Max Wall, who had learnt from the music hall legend Little Tich and had worked in Paris with Grock, the king of clowns. Best known for his eccentric dancing, Wall was also one of the first to deconstruct comedy as part of his routine, commenting on the success or failure of his jokes and ruminating – often with a sense of distaste and weary disdain – on the trade of being a comedian, in the same way that glam spent so much of its time reflecting on the nature of stardom. Further extending the connections between music hall and high art, Wall took the title role in a 1966 West End production of Alfred Jarry's *Ubu Roi* (with set designs by David Hockney), and was later to star in John Osborne's *The Entertainer* and Samuel Beckett's *Waiting for Godot* and *Krapp's Last Tapes*. He was also the support act on Mott the Hoople's 1972 British tour, along with a knife-thrower and a troupe of performing dogs (though the latter only lasted for two gigs, since the conditions on the tour bus, while suitable for musicians, were deemed unacceptable for animals). The same year, Rod Stewart toured America with 'a company of acrobats, clowns and trapeze artists',[49] amongst them Ming Wong, 'who strips off fifteen kimonos while suspended 100 feet above the stage by her hair'.[50]

These elements were not unknown in 1960s rock. One of those names mentioned by Bowie, Nat Jackley, had appeared in the Beatles' television film *Magical Mystery Tour*, while Paul McCartney's 'When I'm Sixty-Four' (written in the late 1950s but not recorded until *Sgt Pepper's Lonely Hearts Club Band*) was not far from George Formby's territory. That album's 'Being for the Benefit of Mr Kite!' had also ventured into the world of the circus, while the idea of a rock and roll circus had been conceived in 1968 by the Rolling Stones for an aborted television show, even if the circus element amounted to little more than the staging in a big top. But these had seemed like peripheral manifestations of psychedelic exuberance, rather than an integral part of pop's identity. Glam, on the other

hand, embraced the music hall, the circus and the fairground as part of the core curriculum of rock and roll. Likewise the Beatles' song 'Honey Pie' felt like mere 1920s pastiche when compared to the 1930s big band sounds used by the Sensational Alex Harvey Band's 'Sergeant Fury' or Sparks' 'Looks Looks Looks', both of which commented – however obliquely – on the decade that the music evoked.

Such influences were initially rarer in America, though they were evident early on in Alice Cooper, a group containing more than its fair share of art students and with a suitably conceptual approach to rock and roll. 'We were more of a showbiz band than a musical band,' noted Michael Bruce,[51] a description borne out by the group's increasingly elaborate theatrical stagings, and by its ability to switch between hard rock and a menacing cabaret, with strong elements of 1930s horror movies and *West Side Story*. As glam opened up new possibilities, other American artists were also to venture further afield, and the influence of the Broadway musical was felt, most notably in the work of Jobriath and Another Pretty Face, but for the most part the impetus came from Britain, frequently feeding back images of a mythical America that had been acquired in youth.

And to this transatlantic trade route in influences there was added a subsidiary connection to Europe. Glam was hugely popular on the Continent and, even if few native acts emerged, there was a strong line in exporting existing culture: the Commedia dell'Arte, Jacques Brel, and Weimar cabaret all became vital source material. The very heart of glam was a desire to play with ideas of drama and decadence, sexuality and showmanship, and it took its influences from whichever traditions it could find that shared the same values.

Advertising for a drummer in 1971, Roxy Music described themselves as an 'avant-rock group',[52] a novel expression at the time. Clearly it was intended to mean that this was a rock band who considered themselves avant-garde, but a more literal reading – that the group pre-dated rock – also made sense, particularly after Bryan Ferry's first solo album in 1973, the title track of which, 'These Foolish Things', was a song made famous by the pre-war British cabaret star Leslie 'Hutch' Hutchinson. It was an indication of how widely glam was prepared to range, as it sought inspiration and allies in its crusade for aesthetic rearmament.

Comedian Max Wall supported Mott the Hoople
on tour in 1972.

Early British rock stars Johnny Kidd (left)
and Billy Fury (right), the latter pictured with
Heinz Burt on bass, whose look was echoed
by David Bowie in the 1980s.
Photographs by Harry Hammond.
V&A: S.12524-2009 and S.11448-2009.

WHEN YOU ROCK AND ROLL WITH ME

'A Little Richard goes a long, long way,'
sang Jobriath, and if there was a founding
father of glam, it was, acknowledged
Andrew Matheson of the Hollywood Brats,
the whooping screeching Georgia Peach
himself, paint-brush eyeliner, industrial-
strength hairspray, pancake foundation
slathered on seemingly with a bricklayer's
trowel.'

Little Richard arrived in the British charts
at the end of 1956, a year that had already
seen the release of the film Rock Around
the Clock and hits for Elvis Presley and
Gene Vincent. Nothing, though, had quite
prepared the British public for the anarchic

onslaught of 'Rip It Up', 'Long Tall Sally'
and 'Tutti Frutti'. Little Richard sounded
like nothing else on earth and, what's more,
turned out to look like no one else either –
beautiful, sexually ambiguous, mysterious,
bombastic, bold and heavily made up. Little Richard
was a long way from conventional
images [...]

was that he was the very first rock and
roll artist making it clear that there was
something dangerous and camp about
rock and roll. There was nothing remotely
androgynous about the macho, hip-swivelling
swagger of Elvis [...]

extrovert – 'I'm the bronze Liberace,' he
proclaimed – and his endless boasting and
attitude – in the tradition of American
wrestlers like Gorgeous George – helped to
[...]

[...] first time I heard Little Richard
I thought, Christ [...]
[...] to get this much sex [...]
[...] knowing it was only a piece of
plastic. Amongst those similarly touched
[was] David Bowie, who was inspired to take
up the saxophone while the songs became
standards of modern pop. The people
covering Keep A-Knockin', Slade covered
Get It On, Mud, Holly, and Jim Curry

Glam drew on Gene Vincent (top left), Elvis Presley (top right), pictured in a $10,000 Nudie of Hollywood gold lamé suit, and Little Richard (right), seen here at the 1972 Wembley Rock and Roll Show. Top left and right photographs by Harry Hammond. V&A: S.16019-2009 and S.14540-2009.

auditioned for *The Rocky Horror Show* with one of his numbers. Even Bryan Ferry, as he stood side-on to the piano in the early days of Roxy Music, seemed to have borrowed something from him.

Bowie's stance on stage, meanwhile, was inspired by Gene Vincent, who had damaged his leg in a motorbike accident. When he arrived in Britain in 1959, the television producer Jack Good insisted that Vincent dress completely in black leather, and urged him to emphasize his limp. 'To crouch at the mike,' wrote Bowie, 'he had to shove his injured leg out behind him to what I thought great theatrical effect. This

rock stance became position number one for the embryonic Ziggy.'[5]

There was nothing that Britain could offer in the 1950s to rival such figures, but even so there were precursors to glam to be found in Billy Fury's gold suits and Johnny Kidd's piratical posing. And, despite the limitations imposed by the Light Programme, there were some disturbing images to be found for those

who looked hard enough. Roxy Music's song 'In Every Dream Home a Heartache' won plaudits for its bold theme of a man infatuated with an inflatable woman, but Cliff Richard had been there fourteen years earlier. 'Living Doll', claimed its writer Lionel Bart, was inspired by a doll 'available for 10 shillings from an address in Gray's Inn Road'.[6]

1 A TALL HAT AND A TATTOOED GOWN

We used to get boots made at Ken Todds in Kensington Market and he started making boots with a double layer of leather on the sole. So we thought, why not make double as much leather and have an even bigger sole with stacked heels?

Dale Griffin, Mott the Hoople

Alice Cooper performing 'School's Out' on
Top of the Pops **in 1972.**

Interviewed in 1973, Mick Jagger looked back wistfully to the days when the future still seemed full of optimism: 'I do feel sad, yes definitely sad that the spiritual thing, the change of '68 does not seem to have gone anywhere.'[1] He was recalling the year of the Prague Spring, of the French general strike, of anti-Vietnam protests. It was also the year that ended with Soviet tanks occupying Czechoslovakia, with the party of General de Gaulle having won a massive victory in elections to the National Assembly, and with Richard Nixon as the president-elect of an America traumatized by the murders of Robert Kennedy and Martin Luther King. In Britain events were less dramatic, but there was still a discernible change in mood, seen in the popular support for Enoch Powell's 'rivers of blood' speech opposing immigration. In short, 1968 was the year in which the forward march of liberalism was halted by a right-wing backlash, after more than a decade of having things pretty much its own way.

That period had also seen the transformation of rock and roll. Fuelled by British art schools, American drugs and internationalist politics, it had developed a campaigning conscience even as it explored ever more florid forms of expression. Now it too faced a backlash, with an invasion of the charts in 1967 by middle-of-the-road balladeers. The three biggest-selling singles in Britain in that year of flower power and *Sgt Pepper* were all released by Engelbert Humperdinck, though Tom Jones, Val Doonican and Vince Hill scored highly as well; the most successful single by a Liverpool act was not the Beatles' 'All You Need Is Love', but 'There

Humphrey Lyttleton's trad jazz hit 'Bad Penny Blues' from a decade earlier – and the Rolling Stones signalled the end of their psychedelic dalliance with the release of 'Jumping Jack Flash'. It was now too that the blues-rock movement began to gain traction. Across the board there was a sense of the mainstream abandoning the cause of experimentation.

At the same time came a withdrawal from politics. The Beatles' 'While My Guitar Gently Weeps' and the Stones' 'Street Fighting Man' reached a single conclusion: society had failed to listen to the voices of progressive wisdom, and refuge from a fallen world could only be found in rock and roll. In some cases the awakening was ruder than in others. Detroit group the MC5 played as part of the demonstrations outside the 1968 Democratic National Convention in Chicago, and were present when the police rioted against the protestors. 'When I saw all those cops,' shuddered the band's drummer, Dennis Thompson, 'the only thing I could think was, Jesus Christ, if this is the revolution, we lost.'[2]

Here were the seeds of glam's own fatalism, its studied abstention from politics. 'The world is doomed,' pronounced David Bowie in 1971. 'We're not capable of making it any better.'[3] Much of his work in the glam era was to reiterate the point. 'Bevan tried to change the nation,' he sang, looking back to the Jerusalem-builders of the post-war Labour Party, before concluding that: 'I could make a transformation as a rock and roll star.'[4] Or, as he summarized his position on 'All the Young Dudes': 'We never got it off on that revolution stuff.'[5] In 1973 Bryan Ferry covered 'A Hard Rain's a-Gonna Fall', the Dylan song that had been the radical soundtrack to the 1962 Cuban missile crisis, and turned it from an acoustic protest number into a driving piece of rock and roll. 'It's very serious,' Ferry insisted of his version, when he faced criticism for trivializing such a venerable shibboleth. 'I think it's a beautiful song, although I can't be bothered with all that Cuban crisis stuff.'[6]

Ian Hunter was equally dismissive of the various Trotskyist and Maoist sects that were fragmenting the far left in the wake of 1968. 'If people want revolution then they should join an organized party en bloc instead of sitting on their backsides bemoaning their fate,' he said. 'It's absolutely no use trying to form some little non-entity of a party in a squalid back-kitchen with just two joints and ten bob between you.'[7] The back of the album sleeve for *Mott* featured the poem 'A Sane Revolution', written by D.H. Lawrence shortly after the General Strike of 1926:

Poster for the boutique Granny Takes a Trip, mid-1960s.
Designed by Michael English for Hapshash and the Coloured Coat.
V&A: E.1698–1991.

Must Be a Way' by the 1950s pre-rock singer Frankie Vaughan. Meanwhile, some of the most celebrated pieces of British psychedelia – Tomorrow's 'My White Bicycle', the Pretty Things' 'Defecting Grey' – failed to chart at all. It appeared that, just as political liberalism was finding that the people were drifting away from the cause, so too was rock losing its appeal for a wider constituency.

The response on the part of the world's leading acts was to go back to basics. Bob Dylan returned to his acoustic roots on *John Wesley Harding*, the Beatles released 'Lady Madonna' – a rock and roll song that bore a strong resemblance to

Tyrannosaurus Rex

My people were fair and had sky in their hair...
But now they're content to wear stars on their brows

Sleeve of the 1968 debut album by Tyrannosaurus Rex.
Artwork by George Underwood.

Don't do it for the working classes.
Do it so that we can all of us be little aristocracies
    on our own
and kick our heels like jolly escaped asses.

For the most part, the position of glam was that society was doomed and that the answer, in the words of Roxy Music, lay in 'a danceable solution to teenage revolution'.[8] Bowie's first glam hit, 'Starman', placed him in the position of a priest, receiving and transmitting the words of an extraterrestrial messiah whose message to the world was simple abandon: 'Let the children boogie.'[9]

Disillusionment with organized politics – whether of the orthodox or the revolutionary variety – was not the whole story, however. In 1969 the feminist Carol Hanisch had produced a new formulation, 'the personal is political', pointing the way forward for the left in the forthcoming decade. The new times were symbolized by the Stonewall riots of the same year, when homosexuals fought back against a police raid on the Stonewall Inn, a gay bar in New York City, an event that prompted the founding of the Gay Liberation Front. That initiative arrived in Britain in 1970, at around the time a solicitor's clerk named Michael de Gruchy was murdered on Wimbledon Common by a gang of twelve teenagers, a crime that introduced the expression 'queer-bashing' to the British media. That was an extreme case, but despite the passing of the Sexual Offences Act of 1967, the public acceptance of sexual minorities was still a long way off. Even Ian Harvey, a former minister who resigned from Parliament in 1958 after being arrested in the company of a guardsman in St James's Park, was still arguing in 1972 that homosexuals should not seek election as MPs 'because public life imposes conditions which must be acceptable to the majority opinion'.[10]

It was not entirely coincidental that the first Gay Pride march was staged in London in the summer of 1972, just as glam was breaking into the charts, for glam had a part to play in the changing of attitudes, even if it was not always a carefully worked out position. 'Our image is political without it being said,' argued Alice Cooper. 'If a fourteen-year-old boy comes home with make-up on and his father, who wanted him to be a wrestler, hits him in the head with a rock, that's politics, that moves things.'[11] As early as 1971, Noddy Holder was jokingly referring to Dave Hill's stage costumes as being 'queer',[12] and inviting interested parties to come backstage.

Much of it, of course, was a playful pose. 'For all that foppishness, make-up and general mimsiness that went with glam rock, there was very little genuine lavender in the movement,' acknowledged Martin Newell.[13] But the very fact that male rock stars now wore cosmetics and flirted with cross-dressing constituted a small act of rebellion against an establishment that hadn't yet entirely come to terms with men's hair falling over their ears. 'A lot of our most solid fans are young boys of fourteen and fifteen who obviously see us

as the opposite of what their teachers like,' pointed out Roxy Music's Andy Mackay.[14] It wasn't always a point well understood on the left, which tended to share the perspective of Eastern Europe: 'This cheap glitter is deforming youths' view of life,' thundered Radio Prague, as it denounced rock and roll, 'keeping young people away from the real problems of society.'[15]

The sexual freedom that became associated with glam had its musical roots, as did so much else, in the Velvet Underground, the New York group whose music was the antithesis to the hippy era. 'I didn't like that love-peace shit,' said drummer Maureen Tucker,[16] and it showed. The band's debut album, *The Velvet Underground & Nico*, recorded in April 1966 but only released eleven months later, broke new ground musically, with Tucker's primitive rhythms largely eschewing a traditional rock and roll backbeat, and with John Cale's viola introducing elements of the classical avant-garde. Just as revolutionary were Lou Reed's lyrics, recording dispassionately his observations of New York's street- and night-life. 'I have made it a point not to be oblique,' said Reed,[17] and his treatment of sex and drugs – including the fact that he sang about heroin rather than LSD or cannabis – was startling in the context of pop music, even though, as he observed, it was somewhat 'absurd to be told you were doing something shocking, with *Howl* and *Naked Lunch* and *Last Exit to Brooklyn* already out'.[18] And, amidst it all, were pure pop songs like 'Femme Fatale' and 'There She Goes Again',

Writer Jack Kerouac, whose work influenced both American and British glam stars.

Sleeve of *Loaded*, the fourth album by the Velvet Underground, and the last to feature members of the original band.

Artwork by Stanislaw Zagorski.

drawing on the sounds of girl groups and soul respectively.

The record was a commercial disaster, as were its successors, but the band didn't pass without notice. The fact that they were at this point under the patronage of the pop artist Andy Warhol was sufficient to attract attention even in the British national press. 'Emaciated jitterbugs, electronically amplified noise and various sorts of home movies,'[19] was the *Observer*'s description of a Velvet Underground gig, even

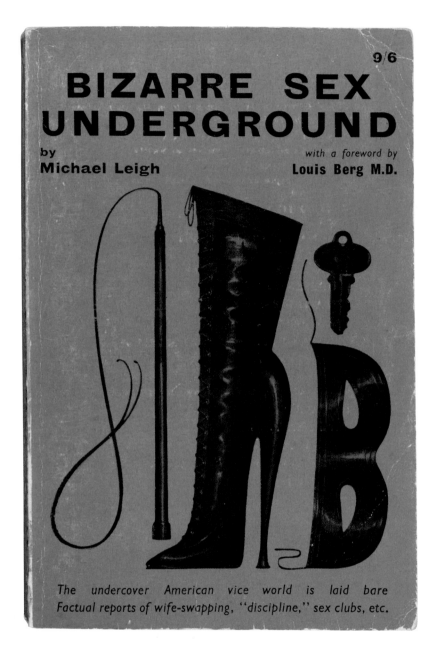

British edition of the book *Bizarre Sex Underground*, first published in 1963 as *The Velvet Underground*, inspiring the name of the group.

Images from the book's cover appeared in the advert for Mott the Hoople's fourth album, *Brain Capers*, 1971.

before the album's release, while the *Guardian*'s Geoffrey Cannon was an early enthusiast, banging the drum for years until he was able to announce in 1971: 'Just about every rock critic has, by now, acknowledged the Velvet Underground is in the top flight of bands, and is the one authentic avant-garde rock band.'[20]

Even more significantly, the Warhol connection brought the group to the notice of the artier side of British youth. 'No musicians that I knew liked them,' remembered Bryan Ferry. 'It was just artists who were friends that had the records, because it was all part of the Warhol spin-off.'[21] There were musicians who got the point, however. The Yardbirds, one of the artiest of British groups in the 1960s, covered 'I'm Waiting for the Man' in concert, while David Bowie recorded a demo of the same song, claiming later that it was the first time 'a Velvets song had been covered by anyone, anywhere in the world'.[22]

At the same time, Bowie also wrote his own (unreleased) song that lifted the chorus of 'Venus in Furs' from that first Velvets album. In its original, this was a dramatic synopsis of Leopold von Sacher-Masoch's novel of the same name, first published in 1870, about a submissive man provoking a woman into acts of cruelty towards him. Bowie's 'Little Toy Soldier' relocated the story to the nursery setting so beloved of British psychedelia, with a young girl winding up a clockwork toy so that it could beat her:

> On your knees, little Sadie,
> Little Sadie, on your knees.
> Taste the whip, in love not given lightly,
> Taste the whip and bleed for me.[23]

Masochism and the narcissistic embrace of suffering was a key theme in glam psychology, as was its religious counterpoint in martyrdom. 'It wasn't only Uncle Peter's airbrushed black and white dirty mags with enigmatic titles like *Spick and Span* that got me going,' wrote Richard 'Kid' Strange, remembering his discovery of masturbation as a twelve-year-old. 'Talk of death or religious ecstasy would provoke exactly the same physical response.'[24] In the same vein, the title of Cockney Rebel's first single, 'Sebastian', evoked the most delightfully cinematic image in Christian martyrology – one that was shortly to inspire Derek Jarman's first feature film, *Sebastiane*, with music by Brian Eno. 'To be on stage is to be a Messiah,' declared Steve Harley,[25] whose other early classic, 'Death Trip' – 'ever thought of dying totally unholy?'[26] – addressed a similarly self-dramatizing theme that was to run through glam, from Alice Cooper's 'I Love the Dead' to Bowie's 'We Are the Dead'.

Even as early as 1967, though, a gap could be seen between the raw material and the way it would subsequently be treated. The contrast between the claustrophobic drone of 'Venus in Furs' and the macabre comedy of 'Little Toy Soldier' was an early indication of the playful way in which British glam would address previously taboo subject matter.

The use of Lou Reed's lyrics was also a display of Bowie's magpie tendencies, as he absorbed the work of others. Such blatant steals were to become rarer in his work, though the influences were still flaunted. *Hunky Dory*'s 'Song for Bob Dylan' was primarily a lament for the 1960s, when rock and roll was a unifying force: 'While troubles are rising we'd rather be scared together than alone.'[27] But it also signalled a retreat from political certainties with a chorus – 'Here she comes, here she comes, here she comes again' – that alluded not to Dylan but to the Velvet Underground, with its echo of 'There She Goes Again'. Just to emphasize the point, the next track on the album was 'Queen Bitch', a song that filtered its Velvets influence through an Eddie Cochran guitar riff.

A decade on from Dylan's debut album, the idea of protest songs had long fallen out of fashion, but the influence of his lyric writing – the heaping up of rhymes, the elliptical imagery – was to be felt throughout glam, influencing not only Ferry and Bowie but also Marc Bolan (one of his earliest recordings was a cover of 'Blowin' in the Wind'), Steve Harley and Kid Strange. It was also at the heart of Mott the Hoople, formed in 1969 by the addition of vocalist and pianist Ian Hunter to the existing band Silence. Their producer and mentor, Guy Stevens, had envisaged a band that sounded like the Rolling Stones fronted by Dylan, and believed that in Mott the Hoople he had realized his dream.

Signed to Island Records, Britain's leading independent label, Mott never seemed quite at home. 'We went against the grain,' remembered Hunter, 'because it was all blues and then the hippie thing happened, and we didn't fit into either of those categories. We wanted to be stars.'[28] It was an anachronistic aspiration spelled out on their first single, 'Rock and Roll Queen', with its premature boast: 'I'm just a rock and roll star.'[29] The early albums made little commercial impact, but Mott became a big draw with a rowdy, aggressive live act that tended to climax with extended cover versions of old rock and roll standards from the likes of Little Richard and Jerry Lee Lewis. They attracted a crowd of 'wild and bizarre extroverts',[30] according to a review in 1971, the same year that the group were banned from the Royal Albert Hall after a gig resulted in damage to the venue and the hospitalization of several fans. They also attracted bad press in France after getting into a fight with the studio audience on a live television show: 'We didn't mind,' said guitarist Mick Ralphs, 'it was great.'[31]

The sense of danger and theatricality attracted a section

of British youth that was feeling disenfranchised by the remoteness of modern rock. 'Mott are the original working-class heroes because of the simple fact that people can identify with us,' argued Hunter. 'They look upon Mott as being real.'[32] The key difference between the band and most other acts of the time was the direct connection with the audience; Mott's desire to be stars was an inclusive dream that encouraged the participation of their fans. Above all, there was the intention of entertaining a crowd, rather than playing for themselves.

It was an approach also seen in one of the few other groups who could fill a 1,500-capacity venue despite having no success on record. Originally known as the 'N Betweens until a record company told them to change their name – 'It makes you sound like you're bisexual'[33] – Slade had built a substantial live following by 1970, with a set comprised mostly of covers. All were delivered in an uncompromising onslaught of rock and roll noise, topped by Noddy Holder's extraordinary voice, a rasping roar from the Black Country that managed to be somehow soulful while still sounding as though he were trying to be heard over the noise of a terrace full of football hooligans.

As they searched for a hit, Slade were briefly persuaded to get their hair shorn and to adopt skinhead clothing, which only added to their reputation as a raucous, boisterous act at odds with the prevailing current of studious musicianship. 'I think people wanna start dancing again,' observed Dave Hill. 'People, especially in the North, work hard all day and when they go out at night they want to be entertained.'[34] The band's manager, Chas Chandler, shared Hunter's analysis of the music's working-class appeal: 'For a period, there were no groups around that knew the same wage-packet type of background as the football fans: it was very much a students' thing. Now it is back to the people.'[35]

It was perhaps this perspective that made Slade an exception to glam's more general shunning of political causes.

(left)
Overend Watts and Ian Hunter of Mott the Hoople on stage, *c*.1973.

(right)
Ian Hunter, *c*.1973.

In 1972, with their first number 1 single under their belt, they played at the Empire Pool, Wembley, as part of a Right to Work benefit organized by the Socialist Labour League (soon to be renamed the Workers Revolutionary Party). But then they also played at 'A Fanfare for Europe' the following year, a concert staged to celebrate the entry of Britain, under Prime Minister Edward Heath, into what was then known as the European Economic Community. 'We're just going to play,' shrugged Dave Hill; 'forget Ted and all that.'[36] David Bowie's contemporary take on European integration was less equivocal: 'The people should be fighting against the Common Market but they won't until it's too late.'[37]

Apart from their commitment to live performance, their love of rock and roll and their connection with the audience, Mott and Slade had in common a belief in dressing up. 'I think Mott the Hoople really did start the craze for platform boots,' said drummer Dale Griffin. 'We used to get boots made at Ken Todds in Kensington Market and he started making boots with a double layer of leather on the sole. So we thought, why not make double as much leather and have an even bigger sole with stacked heels?'[38] As Slade grew their hair back and edged towards their own image, Dave

LOST WORLDS

SLADE · SQUID · PIGSTY HILL · BIRTH
TOM BROWN DISCO · MORPHEUS LIGHTSHOW · BAR — SINGLE 75p
MARKET · BUFFET · FILMS · ETC · ETC · LATE BUSES
THURSDAY 16 DECEMBER 8 - 2.30 DOUBLE 125p

Hill was suitably inspired by Mott to copy the boots, worn with trousers tucked in.

While those groups were struggling to find a way of translating their live following in Britain into something more sustainable, another element was being added to the agenda of glam in America by a band that went through a variety of names before settling on Alice Cooper. They claimed that this came after a Ouija board session in which singer Vincent Furnier asked what his name was in a past life; the answer that came back was 'Alice Cooper', to which a publicist later added the fictitious detail that she had been a witch. Gradually Furnier began to adopt the persona for himself, though tending to refer to Alice in the third person. 'Just like an actor entering into his role, he would take to the stage, not as Vince Furnier, preacher's son and rock and roll singer, but as Alice Cooper, the supposedly reincarnated sixteenth-century English witch,' observed guitarist Michael Bruce. 'I think it gave him the chance to be outrageous.'[39]

From being a reserved stage performer – 'He'd spend the entire set with his back to the audience,' remembered drummer Neal Smith[40] – Cooper developed a trashy cross-dressing act that relied on low-budget stunts, including the ripping apart of a pillow to cover the audience in feathers. On one occasion this developed into an attempt to go direct to the source, with the release of a live chicken into the crowd, an incident that spawned tales about the maltreatment of animals in the show. After a period of hippy-baiting in Los Angeles, during which time the band released two bafflingly dense albums on Frank Zappa's Straight label, they relocated to Detroit and moved into the realm of horror with routines that grew ever more theatrical, as success brought the funds needed for elaborate staging. There was always, they insisted, a moral dimension to their act, so that the song 'Dead Babies' was 'about child neglect and abuse'.[41] Which didn't stop Alice from attacking a baby doll with a hatchet, throwing the dismembered parts into the audience and smearing blood

Poster advertising the Lost Worlds festival in December 1971. The sudden success of Slade – their first number 1 single came in November that year – left them committed to a number of now inappropriate gigs.

over his mouth, as though indulging in a spot of cannibalism.

A key early gig came with the Toronto Rock and Roll Revival show in 1969 that brought together many of the first generation stars, including Chuck Berry, Little Richard, Jerry Lee Lewis, Bo Diddley and Gene Vincent (Alice Cooper provided backing for the latter), though all were upstaged by the unexpected appearance of John Lennon and Yoko Ono, their first stage performance together. The format of the show was later emulated at Madison Square Garden in New York, and then at Wembley Stadium in London, providing the kick start for a rock and roll revival that was to last through much of the new decade.

Also present on that Montreal bill was Screaming Lord Sutch, a veteran British rocker who had never had a hit but whose self-publicizing antics and live performances – he arrived on stage in a coffin and ended with a Hammer-horror enactment of his best-known song, 'Jack the Ripper' – had kept him in steady work for years. Critically reviled for his gimmickry, he did have the support of at least one glam star: 'To me, Sutch was just as valid as John Mayall,' argued Ian Hunter, who had started out in a band with Sutch's former pianist, Freddie 'Fingers' Lee; 'so he wasn't all that as a singer, but his timing was amazing.'[42] Sutch was later to claim that Alice Cooper had stolen his routine that day in Toronto. 'This queen pinched my act and I'm determined to prove once and for all who is really the king of horror rock,' he told the press in 1972.[43]

Whether there was any truth in that claim, the band's subsequent act – which allowed Cooper to behave appallingly on stage before being executed for his sins – clearly drew from the same well. 'What I saw was something terribly reminiscent of British act Screaming Lord Sutch and his funny but extremely silly "blood and guts" pantomime,' mocked Bowie years later, as he remembered going to Alice Cooper's first British gig at the Rainbow in north London in November 1971.[44] At the time, however, Bowie was more interested in the possibilities opened up by the Americans; having struggled to persuade his own band that they should wear make-up, he took them along to see the competition. 'We went to see Alice Cooper and they were wearing make-up on stage and they were really heavy,' recalled bassist Trevor Bolder. 'The music they were playing was great, I thought at the time, and it didn't look too bad, so we agreed to do it. It was a big jump from being in a blues band in t-shirts and jeans, with long hair and beards, to wearing make-up and flashy clothes.'[45] As

Screaming Lord Sutch who, in 1972, claimed he was an influence on Alice Cooper.

Shep Gordon, the manager of Alice Cooper, pointed out, the success of the band 'broke it for people like Bowie who, like Alice, had something different to offer'.[46]

What separated Alice Cooper from other hard rock bands in America was not simply the stage routines: there was also a cheerful embrace of material success that many critics found distasteful. 'Violence and sex sells,' pointed out Cooper. 'We're the ultimate American band – the end product of an affluent society.'[47] He added, in case anyone mistake his intentions: 'I have American ideas – I love money. The idea all along was to make one million dollars.'[48] In pursuit of that goal, the band worked with producer Bob Ezrin to hone their style. The result was a series of classic pop singles, starting in early 1971 with their first American hit, 'Eighteen', a song of teenage frustration and confusion, sung in the sneering voice of 1960s garage rock, which resolves itself into a great cry of defiant self-assertion: 'I'm eighteen and I like it.'[49]

Alice Cooper's 'Hello Hooray', 1973.

Poster for a 1970 Kinks concert.
V&A: S.744–2010.

If 'Eighteen' announced the arrival of a new generation of American rock, the tide in Britain had also begun to turn, with a couple of records that laid the foundations for glam's success. In the summer of 1970 the Kinks, who had been absent from the top ten in Britain for nearly three years and for over five in America, made a triumphant return to both with the song 'Lola'. A tale of sexual confusion, it was said to have been inspired by an evening when singer Ray Davies went on a date with Candy Darling, an actress in a couple of Andy Warhol films, without realizing that Darling was a transvestite. 'It was the stubble that gave it away,' he later mused.[50] Musically the song was a cheerful singalong number; lyrically it was magnificently ambiguous from its opening line (it's set in 'old Soho', leaving either London or New York as a possible location) to its closing salvo ('I know what I am and I'm glad I'm a man and so's Lola'[51]). It cemented Davies's reputation, at least in America, as a chronicler of sexual liberation. 'Do you think,' a *Creem* journalist asked David Bowie in 1972, 'the whole bisexual scene in England owes a lot to Ray Davies?'[52]

Hitting the British charts at the same time was the debut single by Mungo Jerry, a band formed by singer and songwriter Ray Dorset, whose career dated back to the early 1960s; his group, the Concords, had a residency at the Station Hotel in Richmond even before the Rolling Stones' more celebrated stint at the venue. Having failed to break through during the years of the beat boom, Dorset had by the end of the decade got a day job, running a skiffle-type outfit in his spare time. Their first release was 'In the Summertime', a celebratory take on an old jug-band style so authentic that it lasted for barely two minutes. When it was pointed out to Dorset that this wasn't long enough for a single, he suggested that they overdub a motorbike at the end and then splice the song on again; no motorbike being available, a Triumph TR5 was used instead, bringing the track up to a respectable length for the modern world.

The week that the single was released, the group made their live debut under the name Mungo Jerry at the Hollywood Music Festival in Staffordshire, an event expected to be dominated by the first British appearance of the Grateful Dead. Instead it was Mungo Jerry who took the festival by storm, and within two weeks their single was at number 1 in Britain, where it remained for seven weeks, going on to sell more than ten million copies worldwide. Dorset's distinctive image, with an Afro and extravagant mutton-chop sideburns,

combined with the simplicity of the music, was a guaranteed winner, and the record spawned a host of imitators, including the Mixtures' 'The Pushbike Song', Terry Dactyl and the Dinosaurs' 'Sea Side Shuffle' and Tidbits' 'Jean Harlow'.

Amongst those inspired by Mungo Jerry was another 1960s also-ran. 'Marc Bolan said that he had similar roots to myself – 'cause he was interested in the old rockabilly stuff and Leadbelly and all that, so the wobble in the voice comes from that,' remembered Dorset. 'And he said that when "In the Summertime" became such a big hit, he realized you could have a hit pop song with a twelve-bar. Well, people had been doing that for years, anyway.'[53] Bolan took what his producer, Tony Visconti, said was 'a conscious decision to truly "have a hit"',[54] and came up with a similarly drummer-less track that also needed to repeat some of the material at the end in order to get over the two-minute mark.

At the time, the *Melody Maker* ran a column titled 'Blind Date', in which a rock star would be played new releases with no information given to them. When the result of Marc Bolan's endeavours, T. Rex's 'Ride a White Swan', was played to Alan Price in October 1970, he concluded: 'Sounds like that Mungo Jerry fellow.'[55]

Mungo Jerry, 1970.
Photograph by Harry Goodwin.

HOLLYWOOD HIGHS

A 1974 single titled 'Bogart to Bowie' by the West Coast American singer Kathi McDonald lamented the decline of masculinity in the modern world:

*I see you walking down the street,
looking real fine,
And the reason for that is those clothes
are mine!*

Glam suggested that her concerns weren't universal, tapping instead into an alternative interpretation of the golden age of Hollywood. Bryan Ferry may have posed like Humphrey Bogart, but all accounts

suggest that it was the more androgynous Eno who was the groupies' favourite in Roxy Music. 'I don't believe chicks like really butch,' claimed Marc Bolan. 'Valentino was living proof of that.'

And Rudolph Valentino was perhaps the ultimate glam icon. When David Bowie began to toy with the idea of creating his own rock star in 1971, he persuaded a friend, Freddie Burretti, to adopt the pseudonym Rudi Valentino to front the first versions of songs that would later become part of *Ziggy Stardust*. Like James Dean, another glam hero, Valentino died young at the height of his fame (he was

just thirty-one at the time of his death in 1926), but more than that he was, as Bolan suggested, the greatest male sex symbol of the silent movie era, despite a public perception – at least on the part of many male critics – that he took dandyism and personal grooming to the point of effeminacy.

In his most famous role as *The Sheik*, Valentino was strong and masterful while also being 'tender and faithful', the dark prince on a white charger who literally sweeps away the English heroine. 'I am not accustomed to having my orders disobeyed,' he warns her, and despite her retort – 'And I am not accustomed to obeying orders' – it is evident who's going to win. 'You will learn' he replies with absolute assurance.

But mostly glam iconography drew on the women of the movies. So ubiquitous did the imagery become that even a decidedly unglamorous venue like Dingwall's Dance Hall in north London advertised itself with a poster picturing Rita Hayworth in the 1942 film *You Were Never Lovelier*.

And above all there was Marlene Dietrich. As Britain began to fear for its economic future, it looked back to the Depression years in Berlin and in Hollywood, and it was Dietrich – whose disdainful beauty had proved irresistible during both – who was most acclaimed. When he arrived at the photo shoot for the sleeve of *Hunky Dory*, Bowie brought along a picture of Dietrich that he wanted to emulate; a 1975 Steve Harley press release cited her as his favourite actress; the Doctors of Madness used her recording of 'Falling in Love Again' as their entrance music; and when Mick Rock was commissioned to shoot the cover of Queen's second album, he based it on a still of Dietrich in *Shanghai Express*. 'Her arms were folded and she was wearing black against a black background, and it was exquisitely lit. Her tilted head and hands seemed to be floating,' Rock remembered. 'Very strong. Very clear. Glamorous, mysterious and classic.' The image he captured was revived in the celebrated video for Queen's 'Bohemian Rhapsody' single.

Glam was suffused with the imagery of the cinema, hooked on the silver screen. It repeatedly returned to the unsatisfactory gap between real life and the movies, a theme that was to become commonplace as the West's economic crises multiplied. In 1974 the film *That's Entertainment!* compiled scenes from old MGM musicals from the Golden Age, with an advertising slogan that celebrated escapism: 'Boy. Do we need it now.'

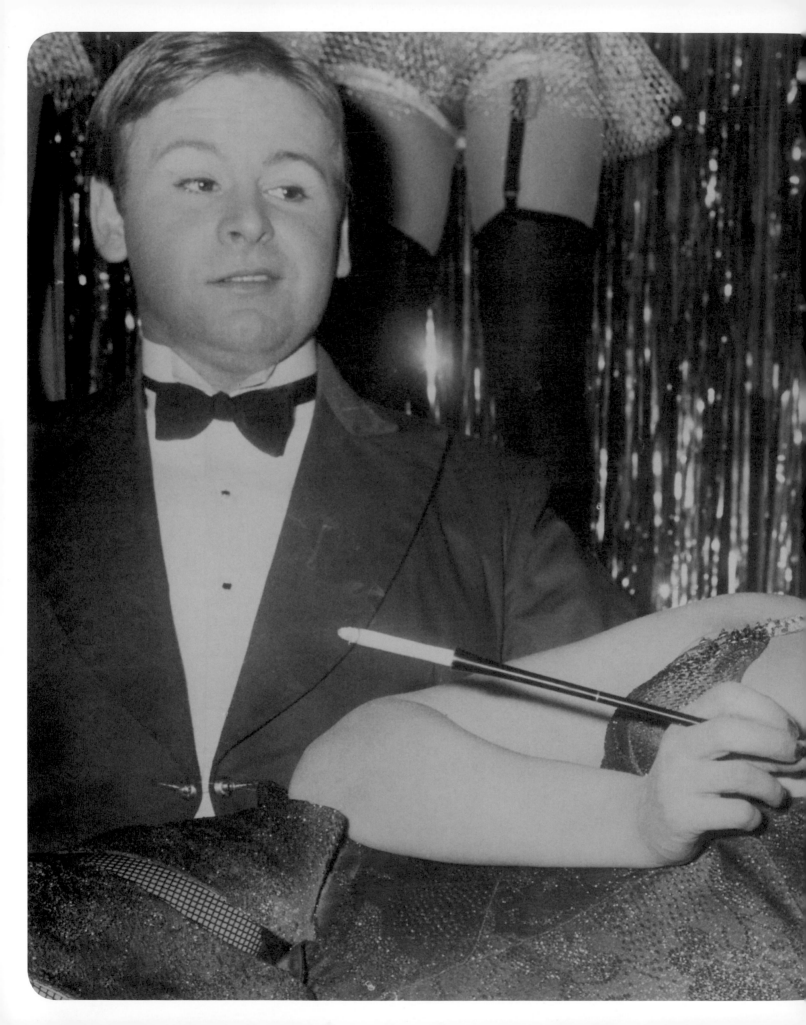

GET DOWN AND
GET WITH IT

We're twentieth-century electric cosmic rock stars! We *should* be projected and we *should* be exciting, because it's a fast world. Whether they're deep or shallow, you take your pleasure fast these days, for everything's moving quickly.

Marc Bolan, T. Rex

Dave Hill of Slade, 1973.

'The mums of this world aren't ready for T. Rex,' exclaimed Marc Bolan, in January 1971. 'We're twentieth-century electric cosmic rock stars! We *should* be projected and we *should* be exciting, because it's a fast world. Whether they're deep or shallow, you take your pleasure fast these days, for everything's moving quickly.'[1] At the time he was issuing his manifesto, Bolan was celebrating the fact that 'Ride a White Swan' had become his first top ten single after years of endeavour as a Donovan-esque singer/songwriter, as a member of mod band John's Children, and as half of the hippy duo Tyrannosaurus Rex. In the latter guise he had, in partnership with percussionist Steve Peregrin Took, carved out a small niche for himself on the college gig circuit and on late-night radio, courtesy of disc jockey John Peel; he had even enjoyed some minor commercial success, reaching the heights of number 28 in the charts with the 1968 single 'One Inch Rock'. Nonetheless, it was a poor return on what had seemed like such promise in the early 1960s, when, as Mark Feld, he had been a young mod about town.

'I remember Marc Bolan with full make-up on working as a rent boy to buy clothes, in and around the Scene Club,' recalled Pete Townshend. 'He was about fifteen.'[2] The ambition, if not the talent, was evident even then as he found occasional work in modelling and as a television extra. 'In February '63 Marc and I went to see *Summer Holiday* together,' remembered Jeff Dexter, one of the leading mod disc jockeys, 'and he said, "I want to be a star like Cliff Richard, I want to be bigger than him, will you manage me?" I said, "Marc, you can't sing".'[3]

The mod background, with its attendant love of soul music, was common to much of British glam. Bolan's London contemporary, David Bowie, was also seen in the same world, which he was later to evoke on his album of cover versions, *Pin Ups*, and experienced the same sense of freedom. 'I've always worn make-up,' he pointed out in 1973. 'I first began to fool around with it years ago when I was a mod.'[4] Both men had made appearances on *Ready Steady Go*, the hippest and most mod-friendly television show of the mid-1960s, where the warm-up man was Paul Raven, later to mutate into Gary Glitter. Raven went on to sing with the Mike Leander Show Band, having moved on from his early rock and roll days. 'We were doing a lot of black stuff, "Dancing in the Street", "Getting Mighty Crowded", that sort of thing,' Leander said later. 'Wilson Pickett, Otis Redding were his heroes at that time, and he used to sound very black.'[5]

Elsewhere, the early incarnation of Slade were covering similar ground in the Midlands – 'We were doing Motown when it was considered underground,' claimed bassist Jim Lea[6] – and further north still, Bryan Ferry was singing in a soul band, the Gas Board, that boasted a four-man horn section. 'There's a photograph of me taken in '67 which is quite interesting to compare with some psychedelic pictures of contemporaries,' reflected Ferry in later years. 'I never went through that at all. I'm wearing a midnight blue mohair suit, with a button-down collar shirt, posing against a Studebaker. I was much more flash then than I am now.'[7]

The attachment to soul was to lie dormant through the glam years, but what survived intact was the attention to clothes, the love of dressing up when in public, that had marked mod out as the most stylish of youth movements. When mod finally broke up into its constituent parts – secondary-modern skinheads on the one side, grammar-school acid-heads on the other – much of that had been lost, the spirit kept alive only in the psychedelic dandyism of Jimi Hendrix and the Rolling Stones (particularly Brian Jones), in an era when conspicuous consumption was starting to look a little unfashionable. For those stars manqué who would later fashion glam, however, material trappings remained very much part of the dream, the external reflection of success. 'When I had no

T. Rex badge, 1973; *Popswop* magazine, May 1973;
Marc Bolan poster magazine, 1972, published by IPC.
Bolan's looks meant that in 1972, in terms of merchandizing
and teen magazines, he was Britain's only real rival to the
American stars David Cassidy and Donny Osmond.

SUPERSIZE FOLD-OUT
GIANT POSTER!

15p

MARC BOLAN SUPERSHOW

May 19 1973 Nº33 5p

POP

All These Gorgeous Gu...
Marty Kristian
Don Powell
Gilbert
David Bowie
In Gorgeous Colour!

★ ★ ★ ★ ★

Popsters Tell How They Caught
The Luv Bug!
and we find out if you've been bitten

★ ★ ★ ★ ★

Brighten U... Summer Wit...
Baubles'n Bangles'n Rings'n Fing...

★ ★ ★ ★ ★

Your fave star~h... wonderful but a ... VERY WEIr... read all about it

★ ★ ★ ★ ★

plus SONGWORDS

money at all I used to dress up in my best suit and sit in Claridge's hoping some of what went by would rub off on me,' recalled Glitter,[8] while Bolan's 1966 single 'Hippy Gumbo' was accompanied by a press release about the artist: 'Likes: $9,000 cars. Dislikes: $8,000 cars'.[9]

That single had been produced by Bolan's then-manager Simon Napier-Bell, who was later to analyze the star quality he discerned in the singer: 'It's nothing more than the artist seeing himself as the essential material of his own art. He devises his own unique image and lifestyle and projects it to everyone around him.'[10] Or, in the words of another influential figure from 1960s British music, the Rolling Stones' manager Andrew Loog Oldham, stars 'have to be so totally obsessed and paranoid about this year's vision of themselves that it's beyond obsession – it's reality, logical and natural.'[11] It was that chimera that sustained Bolan in the seven lean years. 'I always wanted to be a teenage idol,' he was to say later. 'It's lovely to be worshipped and all that.'[12]

His chance came with the departure from Tyrannosaurus Rex of Steve Peregrin Took, who was much more committed to the hippy underground than Bolan ever was. The limitations of the duo were already becoming apparent, and at a gig in January 1969, 'Bolan muttered what seemed to be an apology for the sameness of the instrumentation, hinting that a wider resource of colour is to be expected shortly.'[13] Recruiting a new percussionist in Mickey Finn – 'We just need someone who looks like Steve, the fans will never know the difference,' he explained[14] – Bolan shortened the group's name to T. Rex, took up the electric guitar in earnest and, as 'Ride a White Swan' began to fall from its peak position of number 2, added a bassist and drummer to the line-up to exploit his breakthrough. By the end of 1971, with T. Rex having scored three more hits – 'Hot Love' and 'Get It On' spent a combined ten weeks at number 1, with 'Jeepster' reaching number 2 – and with his album, *Electric Warrior*, also heading for the top of the charts, he was able to announce: 'The revolution has come, it is here.'[15]

Bolan's sudden rise to stardom came largely at the expense of his former devotees, but he was unrepentant,

finding inspiration in the hordes of young fans who now packed every gig, screaming in a way not heard for years in British pop. The press dubbed the wave of teen mania 'T. Rexstasy', and the man at the centre of the storm was loving it. 'If there is going to be any kind of revolution in pop it must come from the young people, and if you ignore them you are cutting yourself off from the life-supply of the rock music force,' he insisted. 'They know what it's all about and even if they don't, they feel the thing intuitively. There's so much vitality and life to be drawn from youth!'[16] For eighteen months, he was unstoppable, irrepressible and majestic, producing a string of classic pop singles that reinvented 1950s rock and roll for a generation born too late to have been around the first time.

Part of the appeal was his image, though the fact that he favoured make-up, draped a feather boa over his satin jacket and had glitter on his cheeks was more about being a star than any great commitment to theatre. 'I wore gold suits and that sort of shit for a while,' he said in 1973, 'but it was a flash. Billy Fury wore them four years before; it wasn't an innovation.'[17] Unlike Alice Cooper, whose make-up was an offensive weapon, Bolan used cosmetics to enhance his physical beauty. The result was a soft, androgynous look that added an element of fantasy to his futuristic rockabilly. 'Bolan appeared to inhabit a mystical domain not so very different from the picture books of my childhood,' was the memory of writer Nina Antonia, a childhood fan. 'There were no scary edges to his splendour.'[18]

But mostly what distinguished Bolan at his peak was his air of absolute self-confidence. He gave the impression of having spent most of his life in front of a full-length mirror, practising his moves. On *Top of the Pops* he seemed too excited to mime properly to the pre-recorded music, and in concert he would pull away from the microphone at the end of every line, as though he were impatient to strike a pouting pose. He believed in himself so much that, for a while at least, his enthusiasm was contagious; he turned simple songs into classic pop by sheer force of will. 'I'm living my fantasy,' he said,[19] and his fans were happy to share it with him.

As the list of hits lengthened, however, critics began to complain that they all sounded remarkably similar. 'That's a load of crap,' protested his producer, Tony Visconti. 'T. Rex have a style, and if artists have a style then it's the same voice and same guitar playing each time you listen to them.'[20] Bolan professed himself puzzled: 'I always say each one is different

Photo magazine issued as merchandizing to coincide with the film *Born to Boogie*, 1972.

V&A: Theatre & Performance Collections.

from the last, but everybody says they all sound the same.'[21]

In fact, he managed to conjure up a surprising number of variations from a limited palette of sounds and chords, relying on his gift for an instantly catchy hook and on his phrase-making as a lyricist. Elton John remarked that Bolan used to 'string a lot of words together that sound good but don't mean anything',[22] and he was quite correct. They did indeed sound wonderful. 'I ain't no square with my corkscrew hair,'[23] Bolan would boldly assert, adding: 'I drive a Rolls Royce 'cause it's good for my voice.'[24] The problem was that, however hard it might be to resist lines like 'a silver-studded sabre-tooth dream',[25] 'you're a gutter-gaunt gangster',[26] or 'the president's weird, he's got a burgundy beard',[27] they were ultimately interchangeable from song to song; in the absence of meaning, there was little to differentiate one from another.

Perhaps this shouldn't have mattered. There had, after all, never been any need for artistic development in the pre-Beatles days that T. Rex evoked. Nonetheless, the critics' warnings should perhaps have been heeded, for once the initial excitement wore off, the limitations became ever more of a liability; the fantasy began to fall apart as competitors emerged in the charts.

The first sign of such competition came in the summer of 1971 when Slade managed to capture in the studio the essence of their live act. 'Get Down and Get With It' was taken from an obscure 1967 Little Richard soul record and – beyond an exhortation to clap our hands and stamp our feet – barely existed as a song, but its irresistible energy took the band into the charts for the first time. If that was to prove more than a one-off, however, it was time to move on from covers. Earlier attempts to create their own material had been unimpressive but, perhaps spurred on by the taste of success, a new combination of personnel, Noddy Holder and Jim Lea, turned out to be a strong writing team.

By November the self-written 'Coz I Luv You' was at number 1, the first of twelve consecutive top five singles, accompanied by five top ten albums. The final stroke of inspiration was to change the title of the song from 'Because I Love You' – 'which sounded weedy', according to Lea[28] – to the Nigel Molesworth-styled misspelling, 'carrying the yobby thing we'd got into the records'. Subsequent singles continued the same disregard for spelling.

As with 'Get Down and Get With It', the intent on many of the tracks – particularly the number 1 hits 'Mama Weer All

Crazee Now' and 'Cum on Feel the Noize' – was simply to recreate the experience of a Slade gig. 'It's audience participation,' explained Dave Hill. 'It's making a row.'[29] The music effectively documented and celebrated the band's existence and, as if to make the point, they marked their commercial breakthrough with a concert recording, *Slade Alive*, that capitalized on the long years of gigging.

Even more crucial to their success was their television presentation and the contrast between the two front men. Sporting side-whiskers that peeked out from his shoulder-length mass of curly hair, and wearing checked trousers and waistcoat or tank top, Holder described his image as being 'a colourful jack-the-lad. I was basically a spiv.'[30] His most distinctive innovation was a stovepipe hat, which he covered

with mirrors to reflect the studio lights; on stage, with all the lights off save a single spot, it was even more effective, a wonderfully low-budget special effect. Alongside this cheerful Dickensian rogue were the ever-changing costumes of Dave Hill, an extrovert who had never tried to blend into the background: 'Even when he wasn't famous, he'd be walking round Wolverhampton in a cape,' remembered Holder.[31]

Appearing on *Top of the Pops* with 'Get Down and Get With It', Hill flaunted a woman's pink coat over dungarees that were tucked into his boots – 'and I had diamonds on my dungarees', he was keen to point out.[32] From there he became increasingly outrageous, hitting a peak with what was known as the 'metal nun' outfit, a black robe adorned with large

(Left)
Sleeve of Slade's German compilation album *Coz I Luv You*, 1973.

(Right)
Sleeve of Slade's album *Slayed?*, 1972.
Photograph by Gered Mankowitz.

mirrored discs and topped with a Cleopatra-style headdress covered with smaller discs, which he wore for 'Cum On Feel the Noize'. Considerable thought went into these costumes, so that when Hill bought a long black leather coat at Kensington Market, he took it home and sprayed it with silver paint in his dad's front room – 'he was freaking out because of the stink' – in order that it would make sense at a time when fewer than one in eight homes in Britain had a colour television set: 'The silver coat used to work great on a black and white TV. Because people didn't need colour to see it, it would reflect.' Revelling in his stardom, Hill also owned a Rolls Royce with the number plate YOB 1, and had a guitar custom-made, with a body resembling a ray gun from a 1950s science-fiction movie and the words 'SUPER YOB' inscribed upon it. Through it all, there was a sense of self-mocking vulgar fun; even more obviously than Bolan, Hill looked like a kid who had been given licence to play in public.

'After a couple of years devoted to worthy but dull earnestness,' wrote critic Richard Williams in February 1972, 'rock and roll is back where it belongs: in the streets, in the sweaty ballroom, the paperboy's whistle.'[33] But even as T. Rex and Slade began reinvigorating the pop charts, there were other cultural developments that would feed into glam. In January 1972 the film *A Clockwork Orange* was released, directed by Stanley Kubrick and adapted from Anthony Burgess's novel of a decade earlier. It was the most influential youth culture movie of the era and the distinctive uniform of its anti-hero Alex (Malcolm McDowell) and his gang – white shirts, braces, black boots and bowler hats, as well as faintly risible padded jock-straps worn on the outside – became part of glam's wardrobe, even if it wasn't always intentional; when Noddy Holder wore a bowler hat at a festival appearance a couple of months later, 'the reviews all said that I had looked like a character from *Clockwork Orange*'.[34]

More deliberate was David Bowie, who was developing ideas for his forthcoming album and promotional gigs. 'The *Clockwork Orange* look became the first uniform for Ziggy,' he later acknowledged, hurriedly adding, 'but with the violence taken out.'[35] He used the film's language in his lyrics – 'Hey droogie, don't crash here'[36] – and adopted Walter Carlos's version of Beethoven's 'Ode to Joy' from the soundtrack as his entrance music on stage. 'There was a distinct feeling that nothing was true any more and that the future was not as clear-cut as it had seemed,' he reflected,

Slade badges, *c.*1973.
V&A: S.1893–2012; V&A: S.1895–2012; V&A: S.1894–2012.

Noddy Holder, *c.*1973.

tying the film to the retreat from the 1960s; 'everything was up for grabs.'[37]

Set in the near-future, there was, for many people, little to distinguish *A Clockwork Orange* from a perception of modern Britain, particularly in the first half of the movie, as Alex's gang engage in street-fighting, rape and murder. The anti-social tone fitted all too easily into the media portrayal of football hooliganism, which had become associated with the skinhead cult. The memory of hippies espousing peace and love, however anti-social they had been perceived at the time, looked ever more attractive in this new, violent phase of youth culture.

Meanwhile, the country seemed to be teetering on the brink of political collapse. In the same month that the film was released, the National Union of Mineworkers had called its first-ever national strike, in response to which the government introduced a state of emergency; electric heating was restricted in shops, restaurants and places of entertainment, people were implored to heat just one room in their homes, and there were rolling blackouts. Mass pickets enforced the strike's effectiveness, culminating in the Battle of Saltley Gate, when thousands of workers forced police to close the Saltley coke depot in Birmingham. It was 'a victory for violence', the then-education secretary Margaret Thatcher later wrote, 'the rule of the mob'.[38]

A consensus was developing that Britain might be at a critical stage in its history. In 1972 the number of working days lost in industrial action reached its highest total since 1926, the year of the General Strike, unemployment was edging towards one million for the first time since the wartime army had been demobbed, and the conflict in Northern Ireland had all but spilled over into a civil war (nearly 500 people were killed that year). All this was against a background of a rapidly worsening economy; inflation, which had averaged 4 per cent a year in the second half of the 1960s, increased to 10 per cent in the first half of the 1970s.

It was primarily this latter development that prompted politicians of all sides to suggest that 'the smell of the Weimar Republic is in the air' (John Pardoe of the Liberals)[39] and that 'unchecked inflation could destroy the mature democracies in the contemporary world as it did the Weimar Republic between the wars' (Conservative MP Norman St John-Stevas)[40]. The level of social unrest provoked further comparisons with Germany just before the rise of the Nazis. A wave of student demonstrations in 1970 made Labour cabinet minister Richard Crossman think that he could see 'democracy coming to an end',[41] while the Conservative lord chancellor, Lord Hailsham, argued: 'Democracy is most in danger when the central ground is simultaneously attacked to destruction by violent and extreme elements from opposite sides. It was this and not Nazism alone which destroyed the Weimar Republic.'[42]

In this context, it seemed entirely appropriate that just a month after *A Clockwork Orange*, there came the British release of the film *Cabaret*, set during the Weimar period. Originating in Christopher Isherwood's 1931 novel *Goodbye to Berlin*, the stage musical of *Cabaret* had premiered on

(Left)
Joel Gray as the MC in the film *Cabaret*, 1972.

(Right)
Vanessa Redgrave as Polly Peachum in the 1972 production of *The Threepenny Opera*.

Broadway and subsequently come to London in the pivotal year of 1968 in a production with Judi Dench, Barry Dennen and Peter Sallis. The movie, directed by Bob Fosse and starring Liza Minelli and Joel Gray, took 'divine decadence' into the mainstream, and though it didn't entirely meet with Isherwood's approval – 'Brian's homosexual tendency is treated as an indecent but comic weakness to be snickered at, like bedwetting,' he sniffed[43] – it was both successful and influential. Its release coincided with Tony Richardson's West End revival of *The Threepenny Opera* by Bertolt Brecht and Kurt Weill, and for a while the imagery of Weimar Berlin became highly fashionable.

Glam was enthralled, revelling in the narcissistic myth that it was living in the last generation before the collapse of civilization. 'There was a theatrical edge,' Cockney Rebel's Steve Harley was later to remark of his music, 'and I took elements from the films *Cabaret* and *Clockwork Orange*.'[44] The Sensational Alex Harvey Band covered 'Tomorrow Belongs to Me' from *Cabaret*, Roxy Music displayed a Berlin influence, most overtly in 'Bitter Sweet', and Bette Midler –

who had built a cult following in the gay bathhouses of New York and was later to tour with Mott the Hoople – covered Brecht and Weill's 'Surabaya Johnny' on her eponymous 1973 album. The atmosphere of Berlin also suffused much of David Bowie's work, from the 'songs of darkness and disgrace'[45] sung by Ziggy Stardust to the cabaret desperation of 'Time'. That latter song came from the album *Aladdin Sane*, where it was subtitled 'New Orleans', all the songs bearing a similar geographical appendage in a style derived from Brecht and Weill's *The Seven Deadly Sins*, written in Paris in 1933 after both men had fled the Nazis.

When, in the mid 1970s, Isherwood came to look back at his younger days, he observed with some irony: 'Christopher was saying, in effect: "Read about us and marvel! You did not live in our time – be sorry!" And now there are young people who agree with him. "How I wish I could have been with you there!" they write.'[46]

If there was a contemporary equivalent to the doomed romanticism and delightful depravity associated with Berlin between the wars, then many felt it could be found in New York. By the beginning of the 1970s the city had acquired an international reputation as a lawless place, where crime and drugs had spiralled out of control and where the middle classes were in retreat, leaving behind a society split between wealth and welfare. 'Fear hangs over the city,' wrote one Briton, living on the Upper West Side. 'I sometimes feel as though I'm living in a frontier town, locked into my fortress, emerging only briefly to fetch children or see a movie, scuttling round dark corners and walking fast on deserted pavements.'[47] At a time when Britain was being dubbed 'the sick man of Europe' – a term originally coined for the Ottoman Empire in the nineteenth century – so New York was similarly being shunned by the rest of America, its image fixed by movies like *Midnight Cowboy*, *Death Wish* and *Taxi Driver*.

Even the artistic excitements of the early- and mid-1960s seemed to be slipping into darkness with the near-fatal shooting of Andy Warhol in 1968, and the premature death of

(Left)
Bette Midler, *c*.1972

(Right)
Poster for the London production of Andy Warhol's *Pork* at the Roundhouse, 1971.

Ira D Gale in association with Lynsey & Haydn Productions Limited and Mayfair Fine Art (London) Limited presents

ANDY WARHOL'S

PORK

Directed by Anthony J Ingrassia

THE ROUND HOUSE

Chalk Farm Road   London NW1   01-267 2564   2-28 August

WARNING: This play has explicit sexual content and 'offensive' language. If you are likely to be disturbed, please do not attend.   **MATURE ADULTS ONLY!**

one of the city's adopted sons, beatnik writer Jack Kerouac, the following year. The Velvet Underground were looking exhausted, worn down by years of commercial failure; with John Cale having already left, in 1970 Lou Reed himself abandoned the group he had founded. The city's low standing nationally was reflected in the responses of American rock audiences for years to come. In 1974 the New York band Kiss were supporting Rory Gallagher in Florida: 'The guy introducing us just got out, "And now, from New York",' remembered bassist Gene Simmons, 'and they started booing.'[48] This might merely have indicated the intolerance of blues-rock fans – Roxy Music supported Gallagher in Liverpool in 1972 and were met with a chant of 'Poofters' and a continual barrage of hostility[49] – except that it was still evident towards the end of the decade. 'Elsewhere in America there's a prejudice against New York bands,' complained Television's Tom Verlaine in 1978; 'people automatically assume you can't play.'[50]

The futility of life in the fallen city was seen in a production of the play *Pork*, based on taped conversations made by Warhol, which arrived for a short run at the Roundhouse in London in August 1971. Bowie, who had already written and recorded his song 'Andy Warhol', befriended the performers – many of whom would subsequently be subsumed into his manager Tony Defries's MainMan organization – and through them found an introduction to the alternative side of New York. On a trip to the city shortly afterwards, Bowie met Warhol, an encounter he claimed to have found 'fascinating' since Warhol had 'nothing to say, absolutely nothing'.[51] He also met Lou Reed and Iggy Pop, the latter a performer he had earlier named as his favourite singer.[52] In the absence of the Velvet Underground, it was Iggy and the Stooges, with their combination of brutally minimalist rock and self-destructive performances, that continued to fly the tattered flag of violence, sleaze and depravity. Coming from Detroit, where Alice Cooper were now based, the Stooges made regular excursions to New York, bringing danger and degradation with them.

For Bowie, such figures had a powerful attraction. They offered a street-soiled glamour that seemed a long way removed from Edward Heath's conservative-minded Britain, where the screening of a television documentary about Warhol was delayed for ten weeks in 1973 while the law courts debated whether it was legally permissible to show such immorality. 'When Lou Reed would talk about the New York drag queens,' remembered Bowie's ex-wife Angie, 'for David that meant that America was the most wide open, wonderful place.'[53] Photographer Mick Rock agreed: 'For David, New York represented the same thing as it did for me. New York was much more obviously depraved than London, and the self-indulgence was on a level that I had not experienced before, whether it was drugs or wild drag queens.'[54] Others associated with Bowie were less impressed; his backing group, reported Charles Shaar Murray, 'didn't seem too much at ease among the Warhol gang',[55] while guitarist Mick Ronson had little time for Iggy: 'Bowie was just *taken* by that crap. I wasn't.'[56]

Bowie's observations of that world were to feed into his work over the next couple of years, but despite his tourist excursions into the seedier side of New York, the influence can be overstated. 'If it hadn't been for *Pork*, there would never have been a MainMan, or for that matter a Ziggy Stardust,' claimed Wayne County,[57] one of the stars of the play, perhaps unaware that half the Ziggy songs – including 'Ziggy Stardust' itself – had already been written and demoed by that stage. For some, the roots of Ziggy went back still further, to February 1970 and another performance at the Roundhouse, this time by a group called the Hype; wearing superhero costumes, the band featured Bowie as Rainbow Man and Ronson as Gangster Man. Tony Visconti, who played bass as Hype Man, claimed it as 'the very first night of glam rock'.[58]

In any case, Bowie's more immediate concern at the time of *Pork* was the release of *Hunky Dory*, his first album under a new record deal with RCA, the sleeve of which saw him playing out his fantasies of Hollywood glamour. For those whose job it was to sell his records, the soft-focus androgynous shot on the cover was a step up from his last release, *The Man Who Sold the World*, which had featured him reclining on a couch and wearing a dress. ('I don't wear women's dresses,' he had insisted. 'I wear butch gay clothes.'[59]) Even so, the image was still a challenge: 'I thought it might be a drawback at a store like W.H. Smith's,' remarked Geoff Hannington, the marketing manager at RCA.[60] To make the job tougher, Bowie accompanied the album with a celebrated interview, splashed on the front-page of the *Melody Maker*, announcing that he was bisexual. Within the world of rock and roll it was hardly startling – the industry had been dominated by gay men since the 1950s – but such facts were not in the public domain; at the time of the interview, there were no out gay men in pop music or in British public life more generally.

Hunky Dory, released just before Christmas 1971, was the first indication that, after years of experimenting with different sounds and styles, Bowie had finally found his own voice and was ready for a serious attempt to become a success. In the 1960s he had proved to be an adept if quirky pop writer, while his more recent work – *David Bowie* (later retitled *Space Oddity*) and *The Man Who Sold the World* – had seen him trying out acoustic and electric rock respectively, with mixed results; *Hunky Dory* brought all the elements together and, on 'Queen Bitch' in particular, unveiled the combination of acoustic twelve-string guitar and Mick Ronson's electric lead that would form the basis of his take on glam. The album also included what would become some of his best-known pop songs, including 'Life on Mars' (Peter Noone had already had a hit with 'Oh! You Pretty Things' some months earlier), though a single of 'Changes' failed to make the charts, despite heavy support on Radio 1, where it was Tony Blackburn's Record of the Week. Nor did the album fare much better; six months after its release, it had sold barely 10,000 copies.

That was about to change, however. For in June 1972, the various strands of what would become known as glam rock came together with the release of a handful of key records and, for the first time, it began to look like a genuine movement.

London production of *Pork*, Roundhouse 1971.

Photograph by Douglas H. Jeffery. V&A: THM/374/1/2725.

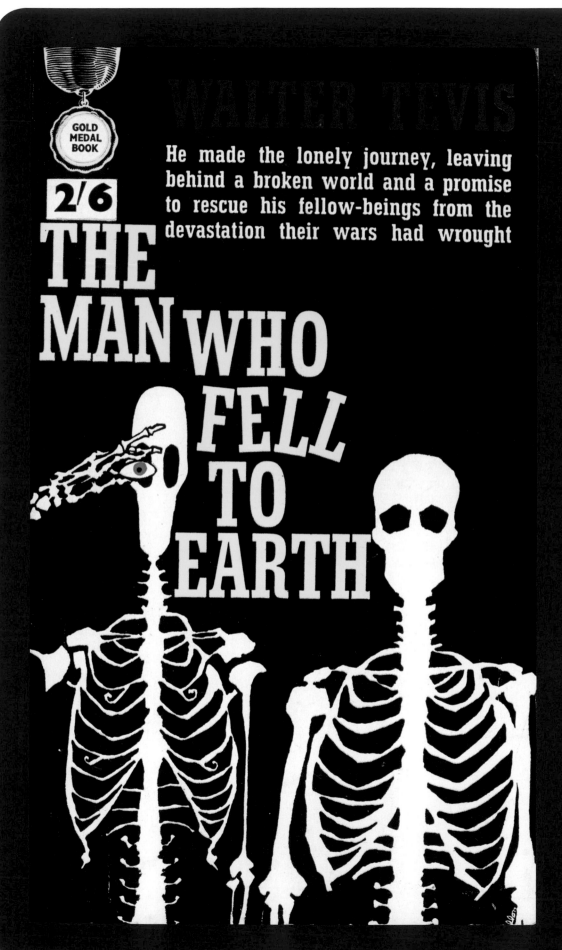

WALTER TEVIS

He made the lonely journey, leaving behind a broken world and a promise to rescue his fellow-beings from the devastation their wars had wrought

GOLD MEDAL BOOK

2/6

THE MAN WHO FELL TO EARTH

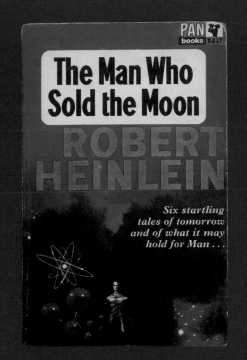

(Left)
First British edition of Walter Tevis's *The Man Who Fell to Earth* (Gold Medal, 1963). A 1976 film based on the novel was directed by Nicolas Roeg and starred David Bowie.

(Right)
First British edition of Robert Heinlein's 1953 short story collection, *The Man Who Sold the Moon* (Pan, 1963).

THE BALLROOMS OF MARS

In one of the most celebrated moments in *Cracked Actor*, Alan Yentob's television documentary of David Bowie's Diamond Dogs tour, a fan enthuses: 'He's from his own universe.' On being asked which universe, the reply comes back: 'The Bowie universe.' Around the same time, Gary Glitter was playing a concert in Belfast, where a gig-goer was asked his opinion of the show; it was, he said, 'like a bloody science fiction pantomime, God help us'.[1]

Somewhere between those two positions lay glam's fascination with space exploration and science fiction. Bowie had, like so many of his generation, grown up listening to the exploits of Dan Dare on Radio Luxembourg and watching as Professor Quatermass battled on television with hostile alien life-forms, and the legacy was never far from his work. His first hit single, 'Space Oddity', released the week before Neil Armstrong set foot on the moon in 1969, took its

title from Stanley Kubrick's film from the previous year, *2001: A Space Odyssey*. (The dreadful pun was also characteristic of Bowie, possibly derived from another 1950s influence, *The Goon Show*.) The narrative of that song, the astronaut's separation from humanity, was echoed in others from the era, including Elton John's 'Rocket Man' and the Glitter Band's 'Where Have You Been'.

Much of Bowie's work in the glam years drew on the same source of imagery, from *The Man Who Sold the World* (its title adapted from a Robert Heinlein short story) through 'Life on Mars' to the figure of Ziggy himself. 'I wish David Bowie were from Mars,' sighed one American fan. 'It would be so sexy.'[2]

Sex was indeed the subtext of much of glam's mining of science fiction. The sense of disconnection, of not belonging, seemed to lie behind Jobriath songs like 'Earthling' and 'Space Clown', and Another

Pretty Face's '(Do You Remember) Planet Earth'. Others simply enjoyed the fun of playing at astronauts and aliens; there was no discernible depth to Paul St John's 'The Flying Saucers Have Landed' or the Washington Flyers' 'The Comets Are Coming'. Instead there were echoes of an earlier era, evoking the spirit of Tommy Steele in 1957: 'I got a strange feeling that H.G. Wells's *War of the Worlds* is going to come, Dad.'[3]

Meanwhile, Bowie's performance on *Cracked Actor* as himself was sufficiently un-human that it secured him the lead role in Nicholas Roeg's adaptation of Walter Tevis's novel *The Man Who Fell to Earth*, a film that, in the words of screenplay writer Paul Meyersberg, was about 'the poetry of the alien'.[4] Released in March 1976, the movie served as a postscript to glam.

3

I COULD MAKE A WILD MUTATION

The theatre is a church. The stage is an altar, and we all face it. And as much as possible, the people that stride about on the boards should be gods.

Anthony Newley

David Bowie and Mick Ronson performing 'Starman' on *Top of the Pops* in 1972.

Vince Taylor never had a hit single in Britain, but he could claim to be one of the most influential of the first generation of rock and rollers. Born Brian Maurice Holden in Isleworth, Middlesex in 1939, he moved with his family to America when he was seven years old; it was in California that he heard a Tommy Steele record and concluded: 'If this is rock and roll in England, we'll take them by storm.'[1] Carefully concealing his British origins in a successful attempt to remain exotic, he became an overnight sensation at the 2Is coffee bar in London, the then-home of British rock. He released a few singles but, although 'Brand New Cadillac' was later to be celebrated, they made no commercial impact, it swiftly becoming apparent that his impressively moody, leather-clad image wasn't matched by a talent for singing.

His big break came in 1961 when he was one of a number of British rockers sent to Paris for a gig, alongside Wee Willie Harris, Duffy Power and Nero and the Gladiators. Also included was Vince Eager, who remembered that when the overnight train from London pulled into Gare du Nord station at 6am, only one of their number could be bothered to get dressed up to meet the waiting press. 'Wearing his black leather suit and gloves and sporting a heavy silver medallion around his neck,' Taylor was received as a conquering hero. 'The day after our arrival, his photo was all over the French press and he received an amazing reception when he closed the show. He was well on his way to becoming a big star in France.'[2]

For the next few years, Vince Taylor was indeed a bona

fide hit across the Channel. Then he took far too much LSD, allegedly at a party hosted by the actress Diana Dors, and lost any grip he had on reality. By the time David Bowie met him in 1966, 'He was really out of his tree. I can't remember if he said he was an alien or the Son of God, but he might have been a bit of both. And he had all these sycophants believing him!'[3]

Amongst those who had seen Taylor in his early days at the 2Is was the future Gary Glitter, who learnt a key lesson: 'To him, a rock and roller's image was everything, and he believed you shouldn't let the public see you as your real self, because you'd never appear special to them again. Much later that became one of my golden rules.'[4] The same attitude was to be found elsewhere in glam, not only with the likes of Alvin Stardust – who made a point of never being photographed

out of costume – but also with Ian Hunter, who noted in his diary as he flew to America in 1972: 'I've decided to travel in jeans and Mick Ralphs's old shirt and my newly acquired Afghan coat, and then change into black leather just before we reach LA.'[5]

Such a mythology sprang up around Vince Taylor, the star who crashed and burned, that it became difficult to separate fact from fiction. One account of his performance was given by 1960s singer Dave Dee: 'He opened his stage act locked in a cage and chained up. Then he'd have two big geezers beating hell out of him with a whip. He was in all the leather gear and the crowd went mad. Then he'd break the chains, get out of the cage and thump the two guys. And that was before he'd sung a note!' He used to tear 'em apart.'[6]

A variation on the same staging occurred at the beginning

The fragility of the rock messiah, seen in novelizations of various films:

John Burke, *Privilege*
(Pan, 1967);

William Hughes, *Performance*
(Tandem, 1970);

Ray Connolly, *Stardust*
(Fontana, 1974);

John Pidgeon, *Flame*
(Panther, 1975).

of Peter Watkins's film *Privilege* (1967), which saw the former Manfred Mann singer Paul Jones cast as the country's biggest pop star, Steve Shorter. (Paul Raven auditioned unsuccessfully for the role, alerted to it by his once and future colleague, Mike Leander, who scored the movie.) In a near-future Britain, Shorter's act sees him being punished for his non-conformity, so that his audience might find catharsis through his suffering, while we also witness him being manipulated by his management behind the scenes. So popular is he that the coalition government – 'formed because of the complete lack of difference between the policies of the Conservative and Labour parties' – collaborates with the Church of England to use him as the focal point of a Christian, nationalist movement under the slogan: 'We Will Conform'. Finally, the pressure gets too much and he breaks down at an awards ceremony: 'You worship me as if I were a sort of god. I'm someone. I'm a person . . . I am nothing . . . you've made me nothing. And I hate you!'

Privilege was primarily intended as political satire and as a denunciation of the media's control of thought in the modern world, but more influential was its depiction of the pop star as a quasi-religious figure, enacting the psychodramas of his fans, and as a blank screen onto which images could be projected at will. Aspects of the shell-shocked star – passive, helpless and disengaged from reality – were also to be seen in Mick Jagger's portrayal of Turner in *Performance* (1970), while much of the shady business dealings that lay behind the rock industry was key to Slade's film, *Flame* (1975).

The influence could be seen even more clearly in the final half-hour of *Stardust* (1974), in which the rock singer Jim Maclaine, played by David Essex, abandons his career. Destroyed by stardom, he retreats to a Spanish castle where he spends his time 'sitting on the balcony in a rocking chair snorting coke or wandering around the battlements like some lunatic Hamlet'.[7] As he awaits his fate, numbed by drink and drugs, he wears an increasingly grubby white suit, echoing that of Gustav (Dirk Bogarde), the similarly doomed composer in Luchino Visconti's 1971 film *Death in Venice*. 'In the last few years, you've been compared with some kind of a messiah,' a television interviewer says to Maclaine, but by then it's too late; he's already overdosed, and as he collapses before being rushed to hospital, he can be heard to mumble: 'None of it's been worthwhile.'

Amidst these various versions of the hollowness that lay at the heart of stardom came perhaps the single greatest act of rock theatre, in which David Bowie created a fictional rock star, then adopted the role for himself and played it in public and private for eighteen months, before he too collapsed under the weight of what he'd become. *The Rise and Fall of Ziggy Stardust and the Spiders from Mars*, released in June 1972, was a concept rather than a concept album (or even 'a rock cantata', as suggested by critic Richard Williams[8]). It depicted a decadent, dying society into which comes the ultimate rock star, who may or may not be of extraterrestrial origin and who is ultimately destroyed by fame.

David Bowie, 1973.

The character of Ziggy Stardust, said Bowie, was named after a conflation of Iggy Pop and the proto-psychobilly act, the Legendary Stardust Cowboy, and was inspired by the story of Vince Taylor. The religious imagery of Taylor and of *Privilege*, the martyrdom of the star, suffused the album, most explicitly in 'Ziggy Stardust' itself, with its talk of the leper messiah and the nazz, a term taken from comedian Lord Buckley's 1952 monologue of the same name about Jesus the Nazarene (as well as the former band-name of Alice Cooper). The most subtle touch, however, was removed from 'Lady Stardust', the demo version of which ended with the line: 'Oh, how I lied when they asked if I knew his name'; on the recorded version, the word 'lied' was amended to 'sighed'. In the original, the allusion to the Denial of Peter would have been unmistakable for a generation in which Sunday School attendance was still commonplace.

For those who knew their Gospels, there would perhaps also have been a memory that what provokes Peter's final denial of Jesus is his provincial accent – which would have been entirely appropriate in this context, for although Bowie's lyrics were largely written in the American slang of rock and roll ('I'm a mama-papa',[9] 'hazy cosmic jive',[10] 'this mellow-thighed chick',[11] 'God-given ass'[12]), his voice remained firmly rooted in London. In the 1960s he had explored this further, inspired by the example of Anthony Newley. 'I always used to like Newley very much, and at that time he was the only singer who sang without an American accent,' he commented in the midst of his Ziggy phase, before adding, 'I'm not overly fond of him now.'[13] The disavowal was a little disingenuous, for he had just recorded his song 'Time', in which the personification of time as it 'flexes like a whore'[14] was an image not far removed from Newley's 1970 song 'That Eternal Whore, Time'. Nor would Bowie have much disagreed with Newley's analysis of his art in 1972: 'The theatre is a church. The stage is an altar, and we all face it. And as much as possible, the people that stride about on the boards should be gods.'[15]

Ziggy Stardust was a startling album, arguably the most influential British record of its decade, a collection of disparate songs that were shorter than those on the previous three Bowie albums, and held together by an extraordinary rock group (who would soon become known as the Spiders from Mars) and by the arrangements of guitarist Mick Ronson and the production of Ken Scott. It came in a sleeve that pitched Bowie as a comic-book superhero, wearing a turquoise jump-suit in a setting that was intended to evoke 'a Brooklyn alley scene',[16] while the reverse saw him in a phone box. (Harry Feld once said that his brother's transformation into Marc Bolan was 'like Clark Kent going into the telephone box and putting on his swimming trunks and cape'.[17])

The record culminated in 'Rock 'n' Roll Suicide', the most dramatic ending to an album since the Beatles' 'A Day in the Life', in which the protagonist seeks in his final desperation the comforting embrace of the crowd – 'gimme your hands'[18] – though, as with Steve Shorter in the novelization of *Privilege*, it's clear that it's not going to be enough. 'When I fall asleep now, my eyes hurt. The bulbs keep popping,' complains Shorter. 'And they keep reaching for me. All those hands.'[19] The record was, judged *Time* magazine, 'a gripping evocation of the fearful doom that can sometimes threaten a rock star'.[20]

The album was preceded by the release of the single 'Starman', promoted by a performance on *Lift Off with Ayshea*, an afternoon pop show on ITV, in which Bowie beckoned Ronson over to his side and casually draped an arm around his shoulders, pulling him in to share the microphone. It was a simple but surprisingly effective gesture. 'Another excellent way of exciting a young audience,' advised a pop manager in Royston Ellis's classic 1964 novel, *Myself for Fame*, 'is to sing with someone. If you were to put your arm on his shoulder, not round it completely, that's much too camp, just kind of resting on him, that would go down a bomb.'[21] Less than a decade on and the audience was ready for the full camp experience. Indeed they were soon prepared to go further and rejoice in the celebrated photograph by Mick Rock that showed Bowie on stage, bending over to play Ronson's guitar with his teeth in an act of simulated fellatio.

Meanwhile, for those who had missed *Lift Off*, Bowie repeated the performance on *Top of the Pops* and success was guaranteed. The single reached the top ten and helped ensure that the album sold almost as many copies in its first week as 'Hunky Dory' had managed in its first six months.

It was in June 1972 too that Alice Cooper made their breakthrough in Britain. Their album *Killer* had crept into the charts earlier in the year, but it was the release of *School's Out* that made the difference. Arriving for a single promotional gig at the Empire Pool, Wembley, they were met with gratifyingly loud condemnation from assorted MPs, educationalists and from the moral campaigner, Mary Whitehouse, the latter denouncing the band's 'philosophy of violence and anarchy'.[22] Concern was expressed over the corrupting influence of the live act, which now included a mock hanging and the ultimate prop in the form of a boa constrictor draped around Cooper's neck. Even more satisfactory was the discovery that an elderly woman sitting next to the singer on the plane was dead on arrival in England; the fact that she had died in her sleep of natural causes was not allowed to interfere with a fine piece of publicity. A memorable appearance on *Top of the Pops* featured Cooper, always a stickler for detail, brandishing the rapier formerly used by Errol Flynn in the film *Captain Blood*, which helped take the album's title track to number 1, replacing Donny Osmond's 'Puppy Love'.

The popularity of that Donny Osmond record had been the only thing keeping Gary Glitter from reaching number 1 with his first hit. Still calling himself Paul Raven, he had spent much of the late 1960s with a group called Boston International, working the clubs in Germany where many of the original rockers still plied their trade, before concluding that his excursion into soul wasn't really doing him any favours. 'I'd been in the wings during a Little Richard concert in Berlin and realized that rock and roll was what I should be doing,' he explained later.[23] Previous singles with producer Mike Leander had always failed, but the two men resolved on one last attempt: 'I said, "Let's lock ourselves in a studio for twenty-four hours and we'll see what we can come up with",' recalled Leander. 'And out of that came "Rock and Roll", which was about twenty minutes long.'[24]

An extract from the track was released as 'Rock and Roll (Part One)' in March 1972 under the pseudonym of Gary Glitter, and got nowhere. The b-side on the other hand, a near-instrumental mix of the same piece, 'Rock and Roll (Part Two)', began to pick up attention in discos and fairgrounds, where the monolithic stomp of the rhythm, unsullied by anything but the most rudimentary music, was heard in its natural habitat. Three months after its release, it unexpectedly broke out of the underground and gave Glitter a hit single after more than a decade of releases, albeit with a track on which his involvement was merely to sing the title and to add the occasional shout of 'Hey!'.

Obliged now to find an image to match the record, Glitter consulted David Bowie, who directed him to Alkasura in the

Gary Glitter badge, *c.*1974.
V&A: S.1892–2012.

King's Road, where Marc Bolan bought most of his clothes. 'Everything on sale there was completely over the top: huge flares, jackets with massive lapels and shirts with enormous collars; and it was one of the few places selling shoes with double- and triple-thick platform shoes.'[25] His moment now come, Glitter stormed *Top of the Pops* with a routine whose most memorable feature was a startled, wide-eyed look thrown back across his shoulder.

Also now making a move into glam territory were the Sweet, who'd been releasing records since 1968 and having hits since 1971. Described as 'Britain's answer to the Archies',[26] they specialized in vocal harmonies and, given the chance, would have liked some rock guitar in there as well. Under the writing and management team of Nicky Chinn and Mike Chapman and the production of Phil Wainman, however, they were initially confined to bubblegum pop, with songs like 'Funny Funny' and 'Co-Co', until the glam bandwagon started rolling. The make-up and outfits became more extreme and the guitars heavier from 'Little Willy' in June 1972 onwards; it

was still bubblegum, but it was a much louder version of the genre. The group even lobbied successfully to be allowed to play the music on their records, replacing the session men who had hitherto been employed.

To complete the impression that something new was happening came the debut album in June 1972 of Roxy Music. A dazzling blend of 1950s rock and roll, shimmering electronica and even elements of progressive rock, the record was dominated by the uniquely mannered vocals of Bryan Ferry. Mostly sounding world-weary and disenchanted, he was capable too of imparting genuine passion, particularly when delivering the clichés of romantic songs: 'I would do anything for you, I would climb mountains, I would swim all the oceans blue,' he cried in an anguished tone,[27] as if desperate to believe in the possibility of an all-consuming love. He liked using, he explained, 'throwaway clichés and amusing phrases that you found in magazines or used in everyday speech – stylistic juxtapositions'.[28] As he was later to sing: 'Throwaway lines often ring true.'[29] The impression given, as he channelled the spirit of Humphrey Bogart's *Casablanca* in '2HB', was of a man plundering the past, believing that the modern world was too superficial to impart meaning to life. 'I don't honestly think that one has the time these days to really be sincere about anything,' he shrugged.[30]

The image reinforced that perception. The laminated gatefold-sleeve featured a shot by the fashion photographer Karl Stoecker that showed model Kari-Ann Moller reclining in a soft pink-and-blue ensemble, looking as though she'd just tumbled out of a birthday cake at a party for 1950s advertising executives. Inside were individual shots of the band members, dressed up with varying degrees of success: guitarist Phil Manzanera and reed player Andy Mackay posed in black leather, drummer Paul Thompson looked ill at ease in a black shirt with a tiger-face print, while the temporary bassist (all bassists were temporary in the early Roxy Music) Graham Simpson simply didn't fit in. The stars were clearly Ferry and the man identified only as Eno, wearing contrasting synthetic animal skins and looking like exotic creatures from an alternate history. 'It's from '50s science-fiction movies like *The Day the Earth Stood Still*,'[31] was Ferry's description of the band's appearance on stage, which was as accurate a description as anyone managed of their slightly disturbing appeal.

This was evidently a different concept of glam to that being proposed by Gary Glitter, reflecting their varying backgrounds – Ferry and Eno were both still at art school, while Glitter was doing the rounds of the German clubs – but there were still points in common: the artifice, the infatuation

(Opposite)

The Sweet performing 'Wig Wam Bam' on *Top of the Pops* in 1972. Photograph by Harry Goodwin.

Brian Eno (left) **and Bryan Ferry** (right) **of Roxy Music, 1972.**

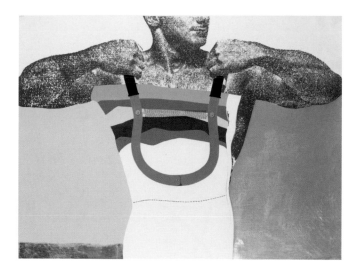

with America, the affection for pre-Beatles pop and, above all, the insistence that the visual dimension was as important as the sound. 'Hearing is conditioned by what one sees,' explained Eno. 'Presentation is integral to how we think the audience hear the music.'[32] Musically, Roxy were set apart from the other glam artists, with more fractured song structures and with a fragmented lyrical style at a time when even Bowie was primarily relying on rhyming couplets. But the intent, the self-conscious creation of an act, was shared.

Ferry's concept of rock music had been influenced by his time studying under Richard Hamilton, one of the key figures in British pop art, whose work was in turn shaped by an embrace of American advertising and consumerism. The traces of pop were evident in Roxy's collage of sounds and words, even in the line-up of the band itself, and in the visuals of the cover. It also informed the presentation of the group, the sense of unreality that surrounded them, as though, despite working in the rock medium, they were somehow not quite of that world. 'That temporary adoption of style and persona was something very much proposed by Richard Hamilton,' observed Nick de Ville,[33] who was at college with Ferry and was involved in the artwork for the first album sleeves.

Others had arrived at the same point. Even before he adopted the character of Ziggy Stardust, David Bowie had ensured that all his album covers carried a picture of himself, a practice he continued throughout his career, using sleeves as a shop window in which he could recreate his image and identity. Pop art had, on both sides of the Atlantic, venerated the icons of popular culture: Marilyn Monroe, James Dean

(Left)
Richard Hamilton, *Adonis in Y-Fronts*, 1963.
V&A: CIRC.59–1964.

(Right)
Malcolm Bird's first design for Roxy Music, used on early promotional materials and posters, 1972.

and, particularly, Elvis Presley, the only singer to have been the subject of artworks by both Andy Warhol in America and Peter Blake in Britain. Glam acts took that tendency and applied it to themselves, reinventing themselves as stars – often before sales figures could justify such a pose – and celebrating the fact; 'like a portrait in flesh', as Bowie sang on 'Sweet Thing'.[34]

It was the philosophy that Gary Glitter had picked up from Vince Taylor. 'If some kid was going to buy a poster of me and put it on their wall, then I wanted it to be a fantasy figure of the calibre they'd never meet on the bus going to school,' he wrote later. 'Gary Glitter had to be a fictional character as far removed from their reality as possible.'[35] Or, as Marc Bolan put it: 'People are really works of art, and if you have a nice face you might as well play about with it.'[36]

In any event, despite later protestations, Roxy were considered part of the glam scene at the time. 'We just want to play rock 'n' roll,' claimed Andy Mackay,[37] and they were capable of doing so with some conviction. 'Roxy rock like hell on this one,' was the verdict of John Peel, reviewing the band's first single, 'Virginia Plain'.[38] They supported Alice Cooper at Wembley and, in the week in which the single entered the charts in July, they supported Bowie for two shows at the Rainbow. 'They were the only other band in Britain at that time doing anything remotely interesting,' reflected Bowie later,[39] though Ferry didn't always reciprocate the enthusiasm. 'There was more affinity with Bowie than with Bolan,' he conceded, 'but we felt very different even from him. He seemed to have been around a bit, and his band seemed very old-fashioned. It was all very straightforward music, even though he was dressed up in a very extreme way.'[40]

Those Rainbow performances were the only time that Bowie presented a full theatrical production of the Ziggy Stardust shows in Britain. Despite the multiple costume

Poster advertising Roxy Music's first album, 1972.

changes, previous and subsequent appearances were essentially dressed-up rock concerts, but for the Rainbow, a set was built and populated not only by the band but by the dancer Lindsay Kemp and members of his troupe. Bowie had worked with Kemp, who was little-known at the time, in 1967–8, learning the rudiments of mime and movement; since then Kemp had become a more celebrated figure on the British stage and had started an eclectic film career with roles in *The Vampire Lovers* and Ken Russell's *Savage Messiah*. His contribution to the design and staging of the Rainbow shows created something much closer to musical theatre than to a gig, and the result was a massive critical success, even if it didn't meet with the approval of all his peers. Elton John reportedly walked out during the show, while Ferry concluded, 'I don't think it worked.'[41] Lou Reed, on the other hand, was in tears: 'I have seen my music played and it was just beautiful.'[42]

Reed was by this stage firmly within the Bowie camp. The two men had appeared together at an earlier gig at the Royal Albert Hall – Reed's first ever British performance – and he was just about to enter the recording studios to work on what would become his best-known album, *Transformer*, released at the end of 1972. The credit read 'produced by David Bowie and Mick Ronson', though in fact it was almost entirely Ronson's work; he was responsible not only for most of the production, but also for the arrangements, the guitar- and piano-playing and some of the backing vocals. It was an artistic triumph, taking a fine collection of songs – largely inspired by the 1960s New York of Andy Warhol – and adding a glam sheen that softened the basic garage-band chug of the Velvet Underground and gave Reed's work the pop treatment it had long cried out for.

The record was a commercial success, spending six months in the album charts and yielding a top ten single in 'Walk on the Wild Side', a song that rounded up all the decadent New York themes of sex, drugs, prostitution and transsexuality. After it had been played on Radio 1 a few times by the disc jockey Johnnie Walker, a meeting of Radio 1 executives concluded that it was too late to ban it on the grounds of unsuitable subject matter, though not everyone was clear why any action should be considered; one producer asked the crucial question: 'What does this expression "giving head" mean?'[43] The track was rooted in the inspired bass line by session-player Herbie Flowers. 'It just seemed a good idea at the time to try putting a tenth in above it, which is a corny interval. But somebody had to do it just once, and now no one can ever do it again,' he

remembered, twenty-five years later. 'Lou said, "My, that's divine." They're the only three words I heard him say. I got twelve pounds for that recording session, and I've never spoken to Lou Reed from that day to this.'[44]

Even more impressive than the welcome afforded to Reed in Britain was the fact that both single and album became hits in America, transforming him from a cult artist into a genuine rock star.

Earlier in the year, before the release of *Ziggy Stardust*, Bowie had also revived the career of another act. Dispirited by years of touring without reward, Mott the Hoople had decided

Roxy Music, 1972.

to call it a day, but were persuaded by Bowie to try one more time with a song he'd just written titled 'All the Young Dudes'. Produced by Bowie, it was an instant anthem for a new generation, simultaneously swaggering and wistful and, if it was closer to Ziggy than to anything Mott had previously recorded, it did provide a commercial template for the future of the band, with the Dylan influences jettisoned in favour of what Dale Griffin saw as 'a more kind of English phrasing like Ray Davies, David Bowie phrasing'.[45] Released in July, the single went to number 3 in the charts, while the album of the same name became the group's first to reach the top thirty.

'People had to get over the shock of Mott the Hoople, the losers, having a hit,' reflected Griffin later,[46] though he sometimes felt that it was a mixed blessing. 'The weird thing is "Dudes" ruined Mott the Hoople. We had a massive fanbase and as soon as they heard "Dudes", all those fans went away. It completely buggered us for a while.'[47] Even within the band

there were tensions, as Ian Hunter began to adopt a more central role on stage and in writing. 'I think they felt the Mott the Hoople they knew was disappearing and a new Mott the Hoople was emerging,' he noted.[48] A new audience was swiftly found and a triumphant British tour culminated at the Rainbow, though sadly the band's original concept for the show didn't happen; it was intended as a tribute to the past, present and future of British rock and roll, opening with Adam Faith and Billy Fury, followed by Mott, before concluding with a new band: 'The future of rock was going to be, amongst others, Mick Jones of the Clash, and they would have been playing punk music.'[49]

Bowie's rehabilitation of his cult heroes continued towards the end of 1972, when he produced the final mix of the third album by Iggy and the Stooges, *Raw Power*. Not even Bowie's name, however, could bestow commercial success on the Stooges, though it was enough to ensure that the record was reviewed in the unlikeliest of places, including *Gramophone* magazine and *The Times* ('his act is sheer

teenage insanity', was the verdict of the latter[50]). The raised profile would ultimately pay dividends.

It had been a hyperactive year for Bowie. In the space of twelve months he had released two albums, together with two new singles, recorded three sessions for radio and television as well as promotional appearances, and fitted in

(Left)
Lindsay Kemp in *Flowers*, a piece inspired by Jean Genet's novel *Our Lady of the Flowers*, first staged in 1972.
Photograph by Douglas H. Jeffery. V&A: THM/374/1/308.

(Right)
***Lindsay Kemp, Between the Acts*, 1962.**
Painting by Robert John Swan. Oil on canvas.
V&A: S.435–1980.

Iggy Pop *c*.1973, image issued on 1978 poster.

IGGY POP

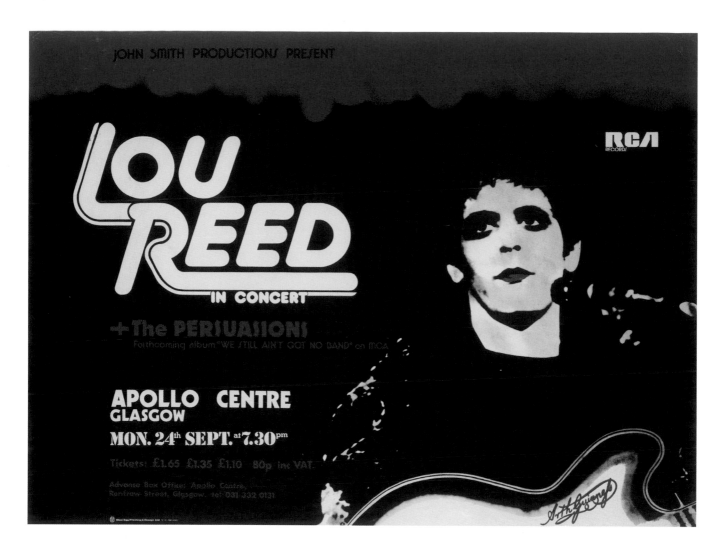

JOHN SMITH PRODUCTIONS PRESENT

RCA RECORDS

LOU REED
IN CONCERT
+ The PERSUASIONS
Forthcoming album "WE STILL AIN'T GOT NO BAND" on MCA

APOLLO CENTRE
GLASGOW
MON. 24th SEPT. at 7.30pm

Tickets: £1.65 £1.35 £1.10 80p inc VAT.

Advance Box Office: Apollo Centre,
Renfrew Street, Glasgow. Tel: 031 332 0131

extensive British and American tours. The fact that he also made time for these extracurricular activities suggested that they had a positive impact on his own career as well as on the recipients of his largesse. He was always keen to learn and borrow from others – 'I daren't even wear a new pair of shoes in front of David,' sniped Mick Jagger, 'because he'd probably nick the idea'[51] – a fact of which he was more than aware. 'I'm very much a conglomerate figure,' he admitted in 1972. 'It's a visual exercise in being a parasite.'[52] His love of rock and roll was evidently genuine, but it seemed self-conscious, experienced intellectually more than physically, and his admiration for Lou Reed, the Stooges and Mott the Hoople – artists who seemed fully immersed in rock mythology – was in part an attempt to find a way into that world for himself. 'I think David was interested in Mott because he wanted to be a little more human,' reflected Ian Hunter. 'Bowie wasn't the kind of guy you rocked with. I think he was also looking for balls, because his rock songs weren't very good.'[53]

And at the time there was still enough of a critical regard for alleged authenticity that Bowie's deliberate reinvention of himself as a star was seen by some as suspect. The *Observer*'s Tony Palmer, for example, took the opportunity of the re-release of *Space Oddity* and *The Man Who Sold the World* to suggest sadly that they 'serve as a timely reminder of what might have been'.[54] In this context, there was something to be gained from mixing with the fashionably obscure. 'David learned how to be hip,' commented Lou Reed in 1974. 'Associating with me brought his name out to a lot more people.'[55]

Lou Reed, 1972.

Lou Reed concert poster, 1973.
V&A: S.4338-1995.

TIMOTHY LEA

Confessions
OF A
POP PERFORMER

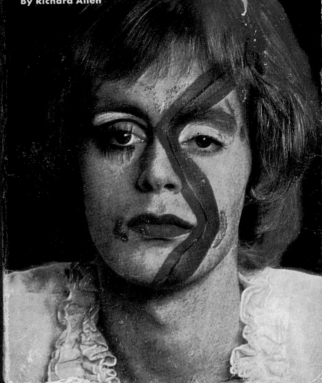

NEW ENGLISH LIBRARY

GLAM

Johnny Holland fights to stay idol of a million fans.
By Richard Allen

BOOK AFTER BOOK, I GET HOOKED

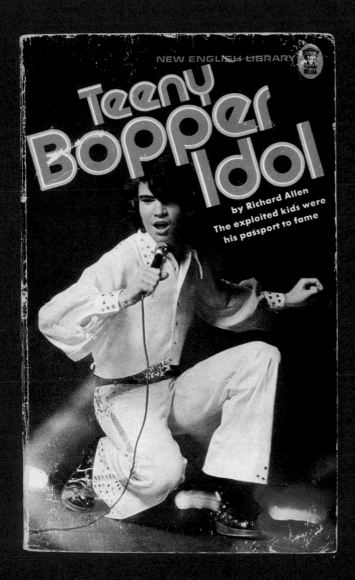

SOME KINDA TEMPORARY

4

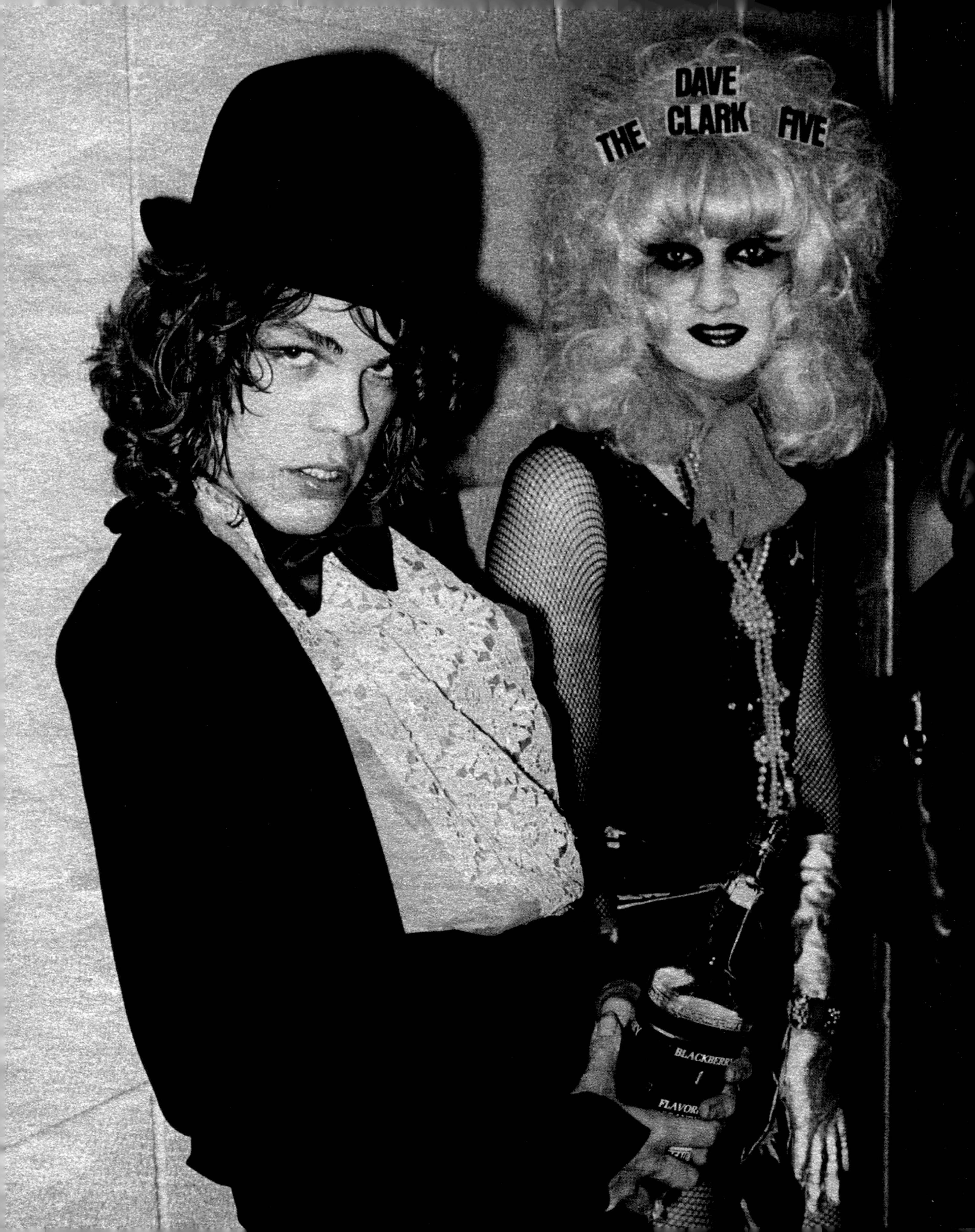
DAVE
THE CLARK FIVE

With the Dolls, it
was just like the street
put onstage. They
were exactly the same
offstage as they
were on.

Richard Hell

David Johansen and Wayne County, 1974.

The pivotal moment in the 1967 film *Bonnie and Clyde* comes when Bonnie Parker (played by Faye Dunaway) has a piece of doggerel published in the newspapers, telling the story of their crime spree. Clyde Barrow (Warren Beatty) is overwhelmed: 'One time I told you I was gonna make you somebody,' he says to her. 'That's what you done for me. You made me somebody they're gonna remember.'

Thus assured of their future immortality, they commit no further crimes and are soon shot down in a storm of bullets, though not before he's overcome his impotence. Now they've been preserved in print, there's nothing left but sex and death.

There was much in the movie that resonated with glam. It inspired, at the most overt level, tales of 1930s gangsters in the shape of Alice Cooper's 'Crazy Little Child' and the Sensational Alex Harvey Band's first single, the wonderfully titled 'There's No Lights on the Christmas Tree, Mother, They're Burning Big Louie Tonight'. More than that, however, the self-mythologizing, the connections between martyrdom and sex (even more so in the original screenplay, where Clyde was bisexual), the glamorization of those living on the margins of society at a time of economic recession – all these were key themes in glam.

There was also a parallel to be found in the commercial success of *Bonnie and Clyde*. The depiction of violence had alienated much of the American film industry and, despite the endorsement of some critics, the movie had come and gone without making much impact. When it opened in London, on the other hand, it was an instant hit and inspired a fad for gangster chic in the fashion magazines. Its overseas triumph was sufficient to prompt a rerelease in America in 1968, when it became one of the twenty highest grossing films of all time.

The first half of that path, at least, was to become a familiar one for American glam acts. Even before his association with David Bowie, Lou Reed had gone to London to record his first solo album, and the subsequent success of *Transformer* became the key to unlocking the home market; a poster promoting the record to the American industry was printed on both sides, to allow the inclusion on the reverse of a collection of articles hailing Reed as a major artist, all of which – with the exception of a piece from *Rolling Stone* (written by the British Mick Rock) – were taken from British music papers. The tactic worked sufficiently well that it became a template for other American acts in search of a more welcoming environment for music that didn't quite fit.

'We concluded that America was going to be a strange place to break the Dolls,' said Marty Thau, the newly appointed co-manager of the New York Dolls, 'so we thought: Let's go to England.'[1] At this stage, in 1972, the group didn't have a recording contract, though they were fast building a reputation as New York's brightest hopes, with a sleazy garage-band rock and roll that filtered the city's girl group heritage through the Rolling Stones, and cross-dressed it in thrift-shop cast-offs and cheap cosmetics. 'With the Dolls, it was just like the street put onstage,' remembered Richard Hell, one of many musicians inspired by the group. 'They were exactly the same offstage as they were on.'[2] Amongst their early champions was David Bowie, who was said to have written 'Watch that Man' after seeing one of their gigs at the Oscar Wilde Room in the Mercer Arts Center in October 1972, and was reported as saying that he 'loves their attitude'.[3] The same month, the band made an abrupt leap from playing New York clubs to supporting Rod Stewart and the Faces at the Empire Pool, Wembley.

Also making a first visit to Britain that year were a thoroughly implausible group from southern California, whose debut album had been released under the name of Halfnelson, but who had then changed their name to Sparks. The songs on that record – and on its sequel, *A Woofer in Tweeter's Clothing* – were full of irresistible pop hooks, with lyrics that were either profound or gibberish, and a smattering of key and tempo changes, all sounding as though it were being played on toy instruments. It made little sense in America, but in a Britain where Roxy Music were being championed as the new sensation, there was the possibility of finding a niche. They were invited onto *The Old Grey Whistle Test*, where the presenter Bob Harris 'made some

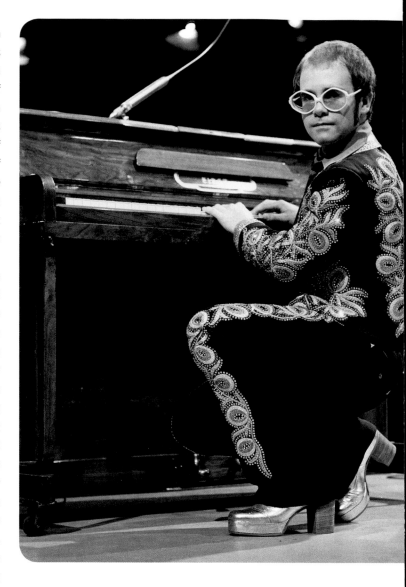

comment that Sparks were a cross between the Monkees and Frank Zappa, which we thought was an amazing description of a new band', remembered singer Russell Mael. 'We did that show and then we started playing a residency at the Marquee and there were lines around the block waiting to get in.'[4] Supporting them on those gigs was a new British band, Queen, whose later cabaret-influenced take on rock – complete with soaring falsetto melodies – suggested that they had been listening to the headliners.

From an American perspective, the appeal of Britain was largely based on the compact nature of the music scene and on the consequent power of centralized media. At a time when the pirate radio stations had been effectively driven out of business, and with independent radio yet to be heard – the first stations came on air in October 1973 – the BBC was the sole

outlet for music, save for the wavering signal from Radio Luxembourg. The corporation's wish to promote new acts was motivated not only by its commitment to public service broadcasting, but also by the needle-time agreement reached with the Musicians' Union, which allowed just fifty hours of records to be played each week across Radio 1 and Radio 2; anything else had to come from concerts or specially commissioned sessions – and the newer the band, the more likely they were to accept the union rates of pay for such work.

Meanwhile, the weekly music press – particularly the *Melody Maker* and the *NME*, but also *Record Mirror*, *Disc* and *Sounds* – exerted a major influence and enjoyed a mostly healthy rivalry, both between and within titles. 'There was a lot of competition between writers to discover new bands,' remembered Richard Williams of the *Melody Maker*. 'It wasn't

careerist; it was more to do with sheer excitement.'[5] It was Williams who first wrote an article about Roxy Music, having heard only a home-made demo tape; his piece attracted the attention of John Peel, who then commissioned a session from the band at a time when they'd played only two gigs. That kind of exposure simply didn't exist for a new band in America. 'This country is weird, man,' commented Iggy Pop in 1972. 'It's unreal.'[6]

(Left)
Elton John, 1972.

(Right)
Roy Wood of Wizzard, 1973.
Photographs by Harry Goodwin.

Diary of a rock 'n' roll star ian hunter Lead Singer for mott the hoople

Ian Hunter, *Diary of a Rock 'n' Roll Star* (Panther, 1974).

found themselves struggling when they ventured beyond the coasts and the big northern cities. And they weren't alone.

Roxy Music had announced at the start of their career that they intended to make it in 'as civilised a way as possible',[10] and had proceeded to do so, using the press and radio to bypass the usual route of gigging. No such opportunity presented itself in America, and a US tour in late-1972 saw them supporting a variety of inappropriate acts, from the Allman Brothers to Jethro Tull, and mostly failing to make a positive impact. Bryan Ferry was unimpressed. 'The New York and LA crowds are very hip and sophisticated, but elsewhere they are literally the dumbest in the world bar none,' he observed on the group's return,[11] though in another interview he dismissed even Los Angeles: 'They were all wearing 1967 headbands and asking each other what sign they were.'[12] Nor did he receive much support from radio, with Roxy unable to find a place either on the adult rock FM stations or with the straight pop on AM. 'We're too weird for AM, and considered too flash and too image conscious for the FM stations,' he admitted, concluding that the real problem was: 'Americans aren't so preoccupied with style as the English are.'[13]

Others met with much the same incomprehension. When Sailor toured the States a couple of years later, they too found themselves playing on absurdly mixed bills. 'We played with cowboy bands in the Deep South, we played in black clubs in Philadelphia, we supported Vanilla Fudge in Atlanta,' recalled keyboard player Phil Pickett. 'And they loathed us.'[14] The group's frontman, Georg Kajanus, had particularly bad memories of a San Diego gig supporting the country-rock Charlie Daniels Band: 'We were confronted with an angry sea of Stetson-wearer punters, aiming their fingers at us and pretending to shoot us, which would have been amusing anywhere else but in America,' he remembered. 'It was like Sailor's equivalent of that moment in the movie *The Blues Brothers* where they're stuck at a country and western venue behind chicken wire, singing "Rawhide" over and over again.'[15]

There were exceptions. Bowie took Ziggy Stardust to America in some style, sailing the Atlantic – a fear of flying was milked for publicity – and playing only high-profile headlining gigs, including a New York debut at the Carnegie Hall. The press there and in some other cities, including

That feeling of unreality was reciprocated by British acts visiting the States, particularly at a time when such a journey was beyond the realm of possibilities for most Britons. Ian Hunter kept a journal of Mott the Hoople's 1972 American tour, later published as *Diary of a Rock 'n' Roll Star*, and felt the need to explain to fans about flying, since he correctly assumed that many would never have experienced being in an airplane: 'For those of you who have never flown,' he wrote, 'I can tell you it's a buzz if you can dig it.'[7]

The country itself was the great dream of post-war British culture: 'It filled a vast expanse of my imagination,' observed David Bowie. 'America became a mythland for me.'[8] For some, the reality was even better than the fantasy. 'New York was way beyond what I expected,' recalled Michael Des Barres: 'bigger, brasher, more neon-lit. I was in a mythic, massive soundstage.'[9] Yet even Silverhead, whose brand of rock came with make-up and a taste for low-life but wasn't far removed from the mainstream sounds of Humble Pie or the Faces,

and issuing a warning about the transitory nature of fame: 'You ain't the nazz, you're just a buzz, some kinda temporary.'[17]

Bowie's next album, *Aladdin Sane*, was even more explicitly a record of his experience of America and included, in 'Drive-In Saturday', a song that wouldn't have sounded out of place as a Mott single. That was as far as the similarities went, however, for Bowie's was a much more jittery, alienated vision of the world he found, one that further blurred the division between him and his alter ego. '*Ziggy* really said as much as I meant to say all along,' he noted later. '*Aladdin* was really Ziggy in America.'[18] There was little celebration here, and the subtitle of the title track – '1913–1938–197?' – suggested a growing paranoia that the Western world stood on the edge of a precipice. With 100,000 advance orders, *Aladdin Sane* was the fastest-selling album in Britain since the days of the Beatles and provided Bowie with the sales figures to justify his pose of stardom. By the end of 1973 he had set a new record for the number of weeks spent in the British

Cleveland, Philadelphia and Los Angeles, was adulatory, but large parts of mid-America didn't share the enthusiasm. Even in San Francisco he failed to sell out two nights at the Winterland Auditorium, where the support act was local hero Sylvester, a former member of the Cockettes drag troupe who dressed like the ultimate glam star but sang soul and funk like the reincarnation of Billie Holiday. 'They don't need me,' Bowie said of San Francisco. 'They've got Sylvester.'[16]

Bowie behaved like a star and was largely treated as one by the media, but it was noticeable that as 1972 came to an end, he had still failed to reach the American top forty with either a single or an album. The more orthodox Mott the Hoople, on the other hand, who had been touring the country since 1970, slowly building a following, had scored a hit with 'All the Young Dudes'. Their subsequent album, *Mott*, felt like a document of their 1972 visit, celebrating the mythic power of rock and roll in 'All the Way from Memphis', while also chronicling their own history in 'Ballad of Mott the Hoople',

album charts in a calendar year: a total of 182 weeks in the top fifty with – at his peak – six simultaneous entries.

Where *Ziggy Stardust* had been a unified, carefully constructed, eschatological vision, *Aladdin Sane* exhibited no such sense of control. Instead there was an apocalyptic collision of decadence and hedonism that went down a storm at places like Rodney Bingenheimer's English Disco in Los Angeles, where a Union Jack flew outside and Watney's Red Barrel was served inside, and where visiting British musicians were welcomed as conquering heroes by the underage groupies who frequented the club.

On the opposite coast, it also went down well in New York, which was establishing a cultural solidarity with Britain, reflecting the fact that both were in continuing economic decline and were both disapproved of by the American government. In 1975 President Gerald Ford's spokesman, Ron Neeson, famously compared the city to 'a wayward daughter hooked on heroin. You don't give her $100 a day to support her habit.'[19] Similarly the administration was said to 'regard the British nation as on a par with the insolvent municipality of New York City'.[20] Much of Britain tended to agree, though it didn't always share glam's fascination with the trend. Margaret Drabble's novel *The Ice Age* worried whether London 'was going the way of New York – garbage-strewn, transport-choked, dirty, violent?'.[21] And a spin-off novel from the television series *The Sweeney* saw Inspector Regan similarly concerned about criminals: 'We can't just hand London over to them and say: "There it is, get on with it." They've practically done that in some places, like New York, and look what's happened.'[22]

While Bowie-as-Ziggy appeared to be immersing himself in the decadence of New York and London, others were looking elsewhere. 'I prefer being in Europe,' said Bryan Ferry in 1973. 'Some of those old cities have kept a quality that London has lost. The feeling here is that everything is gradually running down. There's a feeling of depression and decay.'[23] It was an emotion captured in what was arguably Roxy Music's finest recording, the elegiac 'A Song for Europe', which climaxed with verses sung in Latin and in French, but which hinged on the lines: 'These cities may change, but there always remains my obsession.'[24] If glam was primarily concerned with the American and British traditions, this was a major secondary thread: a fascination with the style of old Europe. 'I had a good working knowledge of different kinds of pop music,' Ferry explained. 'Nearly all of it was American,

although I was also a fan of Lotte Lenya and Piaf.'[25]

Even more influential was the Belgian singer-songwriter Jacques Brel, little known in Britain until the arrival on the West End stage in 1968 of the American musical *Jacques Brel Is Alive and Well and Living in Paris*, which collected two dozen of his songs, translated into English by Mort Shuman and Eric Blau. Brel's sardonic, dramatic tales of sex, religion, death and the socially excluded became a source of inspiration for many, including Bowie, who owned a copy of the original cast recording and plundered it for his versions of 'Amsterdam' and 'My Death' (as well as borrowing heavily from 'You're Not Alone' for 'Rock 'n' Roll Suicide'). When Bowie spent a few days in Paris in early 1973, he sought out Brel, just as he had made sure to visit Andy Warhol in New York.

Most spectacular of all British interpretations of Brel was the Sensational Alex Harvey Band's riveting rework of 'Next'. A 1973 performance on *The Old Grey Whistle Test* was, for many people, the first sight they'd had of the group and, despite the disturbing presence of a violin trio wearing masks and of the jumpsuit-clad guitarist Zal Cleminson wearing make-up seemingly derived from the Joker in *Batman*, it was Harvey's unflinching honesty that demanded the viewer's attention, as he swung between bruised vulnerability and a raw howl of pain. (Unsurprisingly, the record was eclipsed in commercial terms by Terry Jacks's 1974 single 'Seasons in the Sun', a particularly mawkish version of a Brel song that excised the fatalistic wit of the original and reached number 1 in Britain and America.)

'What we're doing is essentially street entertainment,' explained Harvey. 'The thing I didn't like about what was happening to rock was that it was getting too premeditated, too clean, too organized. Everybody was sticking to the rules. There were too many rules. And I don't like that.'[26] Though his normal stage costume was a simple striped t-shirt and faded jeans, he was perhaps the most theatrical and convincing performer of the era, a genuine actor. The band's biggest hit

(Opposite)
Alex Harvey on stage, 1974.

The Sensational Alex Harvey Band, 1973.

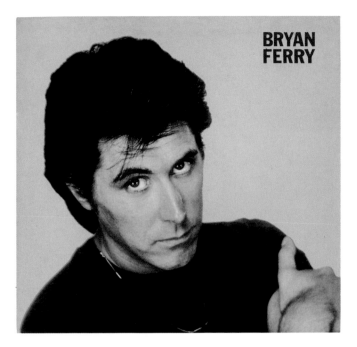

A similar combination of musical differences and power balance saw the departure of Brian Eno from Roxy Music. On the one hand, if America was ever to be conquered, it would necessitate the curbing of the more experimental side of the group, as represented by Eno's electronics. And on the other, Bryan Ferry was unhappy about being regularly upstaged at gigs by Eno's flamboyance, the tension reaching breaking point at the York Festival in June 1973 when the crowd chanted Eno's name, drowning out Ferry's singing; it was their last appearance together. Ferry had already secured the services of violinist Eddie Jobson as Eno's replacement, a fact of which the rest of the group had been unaware until it was announced in a press release.

Sailing serenely on, Roxy then released their best collection of songs, *Stranded*, which made explicit – in 'Psalm' particularly – a vein of religious imagery that had always been part of Ferry's writing. Soon afterwards he was to talk of his admiration for the metaphysical poet, John Donne. 'All these gay blades getting up to this incredible hanky panky when they were young – but who at the same time wrote very moving love poetry until they ultimately approached religion with the same fanatical zeal,' he mused. 'I could see myself perhaps falling into that.'[34] Meanwhile, *Stranded* became Roxy's first number 1 album, replacing *Pinups* at the top of the charts. Ferry's debut solo album, *These Foolish Things* – like Bowie's record, another collection of cover versions – also reached the top five.

Eno's solo career was less assured. 'We want to do a lot of singles, which are the highest expression of rock 'n' roll music,' he announced. 'You need such a density of ideas within the two-and-a-half minutes to be successful, and success is always the key factor of a single. If it isn't successful, there's no point in releasing it.'[35] He didn't immediately live up to this promise, however, and his first release after leaving Roxy was a collaboration with guitarist Robert Fripp, *No Pussyfooting*, which managed to fit in just one lengthy, abstract instrumental track per side. But shortly afterwards came the solo album, *Here Come the Warm Jets*, containing ten songs that demonstrated – somewhat surprisingly – that Eno had not only an impressive gift for pop melodies, but also an endearing, if limited, singing voice. He was, he claimed, something of a 'rock and roll revivalist',[36] and despite the rich tapestry of electronically treated sounds he generated in the studio, there was something reassuringly old-fashioned about songs like 'Cindy Tells Me' (a distant relative to Shane Fenton's 1962 hit, 'Cindy's Birthday'), though regrettably

Bryan Ferry in retro mood, evoking the early 1960s on the cover of *These Foolish Things* (left) (Island, 1973) and the 1930s (1974) (right).

Concert poster from Brian Eno's 1974 tour.

ENO

**HIS NEW ALBUM –
'HERE COME THE WARM JETS'**
Record ILPS 9268 · Cassette ZCI 9268 · Cartridge Y8I 9268

island records

back-to-basics attitude of the music was to prove highly influential, particularly in Britain, to where the band returned in the autumn, though this time with a new member, Jerry Nolan, drummer Billy Murcia having died on the previous visit. 'We have come to Britain to redeem the social outcasts,' announced Johansen. 'We're the tackiest boys from New York City.'[46]

The key London gigs this time came at a newly opened venue, the Rainbow Room at the Biba department store – performances that helped sow the seeds of punk. 'They were perfect,' remembered Mick Rock,[47] and the future Adam Ant was equally taken: 'They were amazing.'[48] The mainstream press were less impressed. 'The Dolls music is third-rate revival rock and roll,' decided the *Guardian*, 'and their act is as dull as it is half-assed,'[49] while the *Daily Express* felt that they represented 'glam rock at its most repulsive'.[50]

To be fair to the latter paper, it was still trying to recover from the shock of encountering Wayne County, a Georgia-born drag queen who had moved to New York in time for the Stonewall riots and was now signed to MainMan, with a reputation, according to the *Record Mirror*, of being 'the tackiest leader of the tackiest band in New York's transsexual twilight zone'.[51] His music was rooted in 1960s garage punk, with some self-imposed limitations – 'I don't like playing harmonica because it messes up my lipstick' – but even more than the Dolls, the confrontational lyrics of his songs like 'Stick It in Me' and 'Fucked by the Devil' suggested that the future was headed in a more aggressive direction than anything Bolan, Bowie or Roxy had attempted. The *Daily Express* was suitably outraged, concluding that County 'will be the death of glam rock. Nobody could possibly take the fashion further.'[52]

(Below)
David Johansen and Johnny Thunders of the New York Dolls, 1973.

(Opposite)
Poster promoting the first New York Dolls album, 1973.

BIBA

RAINBOW RESTAURANT

ADMIT ONE PERSON
NOVEMBER 26 AT 7.00PM
NEW YORK DOLLS
PRICE INCLUDING MEAL £2.50

PLEASE HAND IN THIS SECTION
IN EXCHANGE FOR YOUR MEAL

BIBA-NOVA

Working-class heroes is all right but we're driving around in limos now. We're still working class in that we come from that background – it's just that we're having to change a bit.

Jim Lea, Slade

Suzi Quatro and her band, 1973.

The Yom Kippur War of October 1973 lasted for just two-and-a-half weeks, as Israeli troops successfully repelled an attempted invasion of their country by Arab forces led by Egypt and Syria; the consequences, however, were considerably more far-reaching. In response to America's continuing support for Israel, the oil-exporting countries of the Middle East began to flex their industrial muscles and announced a cut in production. The price of oil rose by 350 per cent over the course of 1973 and continued to rise, causing economic crises throughout the West.

America was hit particularly hard, at a time when the investigations into the Watergate scandal were moving remorselessly up the chain of command in the White House, and when defeat in Vietnam was beginning to look like a real possibility. To complete the picture of imminent catastrophe, the rapid rise in petrol prices led to a strike by independent truckers that turned extremely ugly. Strike-breakers were shot at, hundreds of vehicles were damaged and at least two drivers were killed; in some parts of the country the National Guard was mobilized to protect working truckers, while in others trucks were only able to travel in convoys escorted by the police. 'Supermarkets are running out of perishable foods, schools are running out of lunches and factories ranging from meat packaging plants to car assembly lines are having to go on short time or close down,' reported the British press.[1]

Amongst those affected were Alice Cooper, who were playing an American tour in support of their *Muscle of Love* album, and who were reliant on a massive set. 'For some of

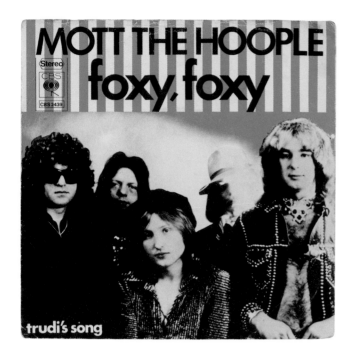

German single sleeves of Mott the Hoople's 'Foxy Foxy' and Alice Cooper's 'Teenage Lament '74' both 1974.

the shows we would get to the arena and the stage never turned up at all,' remembered Michael Bruce.[2]

The situation in Britain didn't reach the same level of violence, but it was perhaps even more desperate, with the oil shortage exacerbated by the decision of the National Union of Mineworkers to stage an overtime ban, thus squeezing energy supplies still further. A state of emergency was declared in November 1973, with major implications for everyday life: street lighting was cut, heating in workplaces was restricted, a 50 mph speed limit was introduced on motorways, floodlighting was banned at sporting events, and television was given a 10.30pm curfew. When all these measures proved insufficient, and with the looming prospect of an overtime ban by power workers and a rail strike, the decision was taken to impose a three-day working week on British industry, starting on 2 January 1974. Meanwhile, the conflict in Northern Ireland had spilled over, and during the Christmas period, bombs were going off at the rate of one a day in London.

These were, both literally and metaphorically, dark days, the lowest ebb Britain had reached since the Second World War. 'The swinging London of the '60s has given way to a London as gloomy as the city described by Charles Dickens,' reported *Der Spiegel* magazine, 'with the once imperial streets of the capital of a vast Empire now sparsely lighted like the slummy streets of a former British colonial township.'[3]

For some teenagers, the good news was that employment prospects were better than they had been for some time. Less welcome was the fact that this had largely been achieved by raising the school-leaving age in September 1973, ensuring that a cohort of fifteen-year-olds were obliged to remain a further year in full-time education. The music industry was also affected; the weekly papers were reduced in size during the emergency, while the oil crisis led to a vinyl shortage that delayed some releases and resulted in much thinner records.

The need for escapism, for some light relief, could hardly have been greater, as evidenced in the singles chart issued on the Wednesday that the three-day week started. All but one

Sleeve of Wizzard's *Introducing Eddy and the Falcons*
(Warner Bros, 1974).

of the records in the top ten were British, and eight of them fell within a broadly defined concept of glam, including hits for Roxy Music, Mott the Hoople, Alvin Stardust, Gary Glitter and Wizzard. At number 1 there was Slade's 'Merry Xmas Everybody', the fastest-selling single ever to have been released in Britain, with half-a-million advance orders. It wasn't a typical Christmas song, but it was archetypal Slade, with lyrics about a drunken Santa doing a 'ton up' on his sleigh, overcrowded family gatherings and rocking grannies. 'I wanted it to be a working-class British Christmas song,' explained Noddy Holder.[4] 'It was also a real antidote to what was happening in the country at the time. We were right in the middle of a disastrous period politically. There were power cuts every day and half the workforce seemed to be on strike.'[5]

The song included a note of hope for the future, but in interviews at the time, many of the glam stars could only articulate the despair of the nation. 'The country has never been in such a state since the war,' said Brian Connolly of the Sweet,[6] adding that he might even be inclined to vote in the

next election. 'I don't think anybody thought we'd get into the predicament we're in now,' marvelled Marc Bolan; 'who would have believed this country would get like this?'[7] Ian Hunter was apoplectic: 'We've gone back to the Middle Ages in a week! One minute it's 1973 – now it's 1073.'[8] Mott the Hoople's new album, *The Hoople*, recorded that January, featured Hunter directly mocking the prime minister, Edward Heath:

Hi, Number Ten, how's things going?
Times are a-changing, winds are blowing.
Big white chief, false teeth showing.[9]

But even Mott were finding that times had changed in a country where the shadow chancellor of the exchequer, Denis Healey, was warning that 'there are going to be howls of anguish from the rich' when Labour next took power.[10] In the politically charged atmosphere of 1974, sides were being taken, and the fact of stardom separated the group from those who remained in the crowd. Arriving at the studio to begin work on the album, bassist Overend Watts turned up 'in my '58 Cadillac Eldorado and asked the uniformed doorman where I could park. He proceeded to go mental at me for owning a huge flash car, which used an obscene amount of petrol and "ruined things for the poor people".'[11]

A few months later, Jim Lea of Slade was explaining to the press why he'd moved to London from the Black Country. 'Wolverhampton has never really done anything for us,' he said. 'Working-class heroes is all right but we're driving around in limos now. We're still working class in that we come from that background – it's just that we're having to change a bit.'[12] Back in 1971, Noddy Holder had been quite clear about where he stood: 'We are aimed at the masses. Every pop band should be.'[13] But the fruits of success inevitably removed the artist from the masses. Which was why Marc Bolan went into tax exile as Healey introduced a top rate of income tax of 83 per cent.

Also recording an album in London that January were Sparks. Full of optimism, the brothers Ron and Russell Mael had relocated to Britain, signed a contract with Island Records and recruited a new set of musicians. 'The vibes were great,' remembered Russell. 'We had Muff Winwood producing, the support within the company was fantastic, we'd moved to England and this was our dream – we were always Anglophiles.'[14] They found, however, that recording was disrupted by the scheduled blackouts that came with rationed

RECORD ILPS 9272. CASSETTE ZCI 9272. CARTRIDGE Y8I 9272.

No 1

power. They then faced the prospect that, even if it were finished, the album might not get pressed because of the vinyl shortage. 'It wasn't part of our dream of coming to Britain,' reflected Mael ruefully.

The immediate moment of political crisis ended in February with a general election that removed Heath from Downing Street and saw the return of Harold Wilson, albeit with a minority government, but for Sparks there were further lessons to come as they assimilated into 1970s Britain. The album, *Kimono My House*, was released in May 1974 with a Karl Stoecker cover photograph of two members of a Kabuki theatre group, a genre in which female roles are played by men. Its accompanying single, 'This Town Ain't Big Enough for Both of Us', sold well enough to earn a place on *Top of the Pops*. At that point they discovered that they lacked the necessary work permits to satisfy the Musicians' Union.

They were pulled from the show and their place given to the Rubettes, whose 'Sugar Baby Love' had been released some four months earlier and been a turntable hit on Radio 1 without breaching the top fifty. Originally written as a possible

entry for the Eurovision Song Contest (held that year in Brighton, where metal detectors and security searches were in operation for the first time), and then turned down by rock and roll revivalists Showaddywaddy, 'Sugar Baby Love' was instead recorded by a group of session musicians and, with the exposure of that *Top of the Pops* performance, rose to number 1 within a fortnight, launching the Rubettes on a successful career.

Sparks meanwhile were allowed on television once they'd sorted out their problems with the Musicians' Union, and they made an instant impression. Russell Mael, with long corkscrew hair and the face of a teen idol, had a perfect foil in the terrifying sight of his older brother, sitting motionless at the keyboard, with short hair plastered back and a toothbrush moustache; his intense, sidelong stares at the camera became even more scary when he unveiled a small, sickly smile. He was, suggested the *Melody Maker*, 'a throwback to Edwardian suburbia with the mesmerizing face of a child murderer'.[15] Their single rose rapidly as well, kept from number 1 only by 'Sugar Baby Love', and within months they were a pop sensation, in demand for interviews by teen magazines like *Jackie* and attracting audiences of young girls who screamed too loud to hear the witty lyrics about marital infidelity, capitalism and Albert Einstein.

By June 1974 the *Melody Maker* was heralding Sparks as one of 'the two major new phenomena of British rock'.[16] The others were Cockney Rebel, a band whose album, *The Human Menagerie*, had been released the previous November, an assured and self-confident debut to match that of Jobriath, though the influences here were less from Broadway than from literature. 'At the time I was into Eliot, Wordsworth, Hemingway,' said the band's singer and songwriter, Steve Harley.[17] Which didn't make it any the less theatrical. The album closed with the melodramatic 'Death Trip', a breathtakingly histrionic, orchestrated epic that lasted for ten minutes and wandered at various points into something resembling the Red Army Choir, while still sounding as though it were documenting the collapse of society. Also included was the band's debut single, the slow-burning ballad 'Sebastian'; slightly shorter but still seven minutes long and closer in spirit to Swinburne than to the Sweet, it failed to make the British charts but spent eight weeks at number 1 in Belgium.

Harley's image, as seen on the cover of the album, was of a very delicate boy, dressed in a peach ensemble that matched his nail polish and the blusher that made his pallid face look as though it had been prepared by an undertaker. His accent was as London as David Bowie's, his singing as contorted and mannered as Bryan Ferry's, though the latter was unimpressed by the suggestion that someone might be muscling in on his territory. 'I think he's trading on a parody of that stance,' sniffed Ferry. 'Also he needs a good tailor.'[18] But Harley, a former journalist, was even better at generating press attention, with a strong line in blowing his own trumpet: 'I always said we were gonna get to the top. It wasn't bragging, it wasn't bigheadedness. I was purely saying, look, I feel like God's touched me and said: Here's a mission and someone's gotta do it.'[19] When playing at Biba, he introduced the members of the band, concluding: 'And I'm Muhammad 'Arley.'[20] Commercial success came in 1974 with a non-album single, 'Judy Teen', that effortlessly reached the top five, though Harley seemed unhappy with lowering himself to competing in the marketplace, describing an appearance on

(Opposite)
Poster advertising Sparks' *Kimono My House* **(Island, 1974).**

**Press pack issued to accompany
Cockney Rebel's concert at Biba, 1974.**

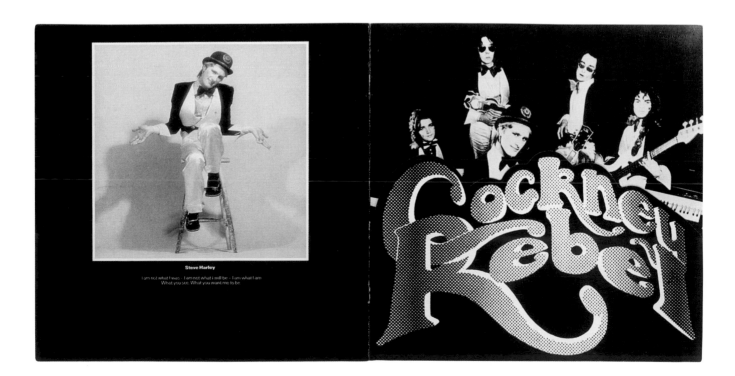

(Opposite)
Cockney Rebel concert poster, 1974. Note the wrong date: the concert was actually on 16 July.

German sleeve of Cockney Rebel, 'Judy Teen', 1974.

Top of the Pops as being 'probably the most degrading experience in the band's history'.[21]

Apart from the charisma of Harley himself, Cockney Rebel stood out by their refusal to use electric guitars, with the sound dominated instead by the classically trained keyboards of Milton Reame-James and by the fiddle playing of Jean-Paul Crocker. It was a somewhat unexpected consequence of the way that glam had expanded the sound palette of rock music, and others similarly took the opportunity to explore, amongst them Slapp Happy, a left-field art-rock band whose self-titled debut album (later renamed *Casablanca Moon*) was a splendidly skewed collection of pop songs; with the vocals of the German-born Dagmar Krause, they sounded like a playful take on the Brecht–Weill songbook.

There was also Georg Kajanus, the son of a Norwegian prince who had grown up in the harbour town of Trondheim, before spending two years as an adolescent in Paris. 'I would listen to Brel, Piaf, Brassens, Aznavour, and spend many, many evenings talking to the "ladies of the night" in the red-light districts of Place Pigalle and Rue St Denis,' he wrote. 'With bemused indulgence, they tolerated this lanky, inexperienced Norwegian kid and on their coffee breaks, they gave me, for the price of a few beverages, some of the benefits of their colourful experiences.'[22] The dazzling debut album by Sailor, the band he formed in London with keyboard player Phil Pickett, was comprised almost entirely of songs based on those experiences, written for a proposed musical, *The Red Light Review*, about sailors on shore leave in Marseilles in the late 1940s.

Dressed as naval ratings, with unfashionably short hair, Sailor further distanced themselves from anything else in rock and roll by using a self-constructed instrument, known as the Nickelodeon, comprising two upright pianos placed back-to-back, augmented by a glockenspiel and synthesizers, all played in a standing position. 'We studiously avoided the rock route,' said Pickett. 'We didn't have a lead guitarist, we didn't have a bass player – we were one of the first bands to use synthesizer bass, which I played – and there were no guitar solos at all, just this Nickelodeon thing.'[23] With just two showcase gigs behind them, Sailor were given a chance to play on the BBC2 show *In Concert*, an appearance which attracted sufficient attention to gain them a support slot on a scheduled British tour by Mott the Hoople in the autumn of 1974. That tour was cancelled, but the group did go on to support Steve Harley and Cockney Rebel early in 1975.

The same television series had earlier provided a launch pad for another of the more unlikely acts that operated in the space opened up by glam. Leo Sayer, with his co-writer David Courtney, had contributed most of the material on the first solo album by Roger Daltrey, but his big moment came towards the end of 1973 with his debut single, 'The Show Must Go On', a piano- and banjo-driven song of showbiz alienation performed on *In Concert* in full Pierrot outfit and make-up. The same visual approach was adopted for concerts through to the middle of 1974, as Sayer promoted an album that was originally going to be titled *The Loser*, before emerging as *Silverbird*. 'I'm a masochist,' he explained. 'The clown never knows whether they're laughing at him or with him. He just hopes they're laughing with him. It suddenly becomes a very lonely situation when they laugh at him. All of a sudden, that changes everything.'[24] The image emphasized the disparity between Sayer's slight frame and the power of his voice, as well as a music that didn't quite fit. 'It went through the roof,' remembered Courtney, 'because I don't think anyone had ever seen anything like that before. They hadn't seen anybody who looked like him, they hadn't heard music that had this strange combination – Leo was a big Captain Beefheart fan, I was a really big Beatles fan.'[25]

Sayer wasn't the only one to pick up the Pierrot image. When David Bowie worked with Lindsay Kemp in 1967, they had collaborated on a show rooted in the Commedia dell'Arte titled *Pierrot in Turquoise*, while Jobriath named his publishing company Pierrot Music. Slightly less plausibly, it was also the first image of Alvin Stardust.

In mid-1973 the writer-producer Peter Shelley had set up Magnet Records with Michael Levy (Tony Blair's future fundraiser). 'To get the ball rolling, I decided to invent an artiste and record a one-off single I wrote, produced and sang,' explained Shelley.[26] Released under the name Alvin Stardust, 'My Coo-Ca-Choo' became the company's first single and, as it began to attract attention, Shelley cast around, trying to find someone who was prepared to adopt the persona of Alvin. Meanwhile, he himself appeared on *Lift Off with Ayshea* for the first television promotion in what one critic called 'a pink and blue confection'[27] or, more specifically, 'dressed as a Pierrot clown', in the words of Vince Eager,[28] one of those invited to consider the job.

Eager turned down the opportunity, as did Marty Wilde, but Shane Fenton – another star of the pre-Beatles British rock and roll scene – accepted the offer, discarded the clown approach and dressed instead in black leathers, creating a strong enough look that the original was immediately forgotten. 'People write and say I'm copying Gene Vincent with the clothes and style of singing,' admitted the newly incarnated Alvin, 'and the only answer I've got is: yes!'[29]

Sailor on stage, 1975.

Both Leo Sayer's and Alvin Stardust's debut singles were in that first top ten of January 1974, as was 'Lamplight', the second hit for David Essex. After the traditional years of failure, Essex had become an overnight success as an actor, a star of stage (*Godspell*) and screen (*That'll Be the Day*), before relaunching his musical career with the song 'Rock On', which he demonstrated to producer Jeff Wayne late one night at the end of a session recording jingles. 'David picked up a trashcan and started banging out this little rhythm,' remembered Wayne. 'Because there were no instruments, the engineer put on a repeat echo, and it gave an atmosphere to it. The attractiveness was the hollows, the absences, so I had this idea that there would be nothing on it that played a chord. That's why there are no keyboards or guitars.'[30] There was, however, a wonderfully simple bass part, played by Herbie Flowers, who had the idea of doubling the line an octave up: 'My reward for that was instead of getting twelve pounds for doing a three-hour recording session, I got twenty-four. Because there's two bits.'[31] The result was a stunningly atmospheric single, sounding like a dub version of Gene Vincent, with lyrics evoking the early days of rock and roll.

Much of the material on Essex's first three albums – all produced by Wayne – was similarly striking, though he, like Leo Sayer, soon reverted to more orthodox middle-of-the-road pop. But the fact that they had started with such left-field pieces of rock theatre was testament to the tenor of the times, when glam had raised the dramatic stakes.

The other side of glam, the more rowdy rock and roll, was proving less successful in producing new stars. The most likely candidates were the Hollywood Brats, the closest that Britain came to the New York Dolls, but they had to wait until they'd split up before their recordings were released. The Jook, a band that came out of Scotland with boots, braces and cropped hair, released five Slade-esque singles on RCA without scoring a hit. Others failed even to get that far. Manchester-based group Smiffy had a line-up that included the future radio disc jockey Mike Sweeney, who remembered bleached blond hair, stockings and suspenders and knee-length women's boots, as well as a set list that ranged from Bowie and Slade to the Doors and Status Quo, and included a couple of originals, 'Intergalactic Boogie' and 'Ringy Dingy'. Similarly there was the Colchester band Plod, whose main figure, Martin Newell, was later to write about the crowds they played to in East Anglia: 'Our audience were stocky village lads, on great four-inch platform shoes, their King-Edward

Inside sleeve of Leo Sayer, *Silverbird*, 1973.

in their hair just for the occasion. Then afterwards they'd wash it all off and go home.'[35] Most spectacular of all were Bowie's followers, who tried hard to keep up with his rapidly evolving look, even in everyday life. 'I remember going to school with a circle on my head, with my hair standing up,' recalled the television presenter Lorraine Kelly, then a Glasgow schoolgirl. 'People must have thought I was completely bonkers.'[36]

Such dedication sometimes came at a price. Marc Almond went to a Ziggy Stardust show in Liverpool in 1973: 'My make-up was smeared with dried blood because I'd been hit over the head on the way to the show for the way I looked.'[37] It was an indication that Bowie's public avowal of bisexuality was out of kilter with most of the country, as Mick Ronson also discovered. 'My family in Hull took a lot of flak for it,' he said. 'Like throwing paint over the car and paint up the front door and stuff like that, which really annoyed me. It's pretty sad.'[38]

In retrospect, the interview in which Bowie revealed his sexuality has sometimes been regarded as little more than a gimmick, a piece of bandwagon-jumping. At the time, however, there was precious little sign of any such bandwagon. There was the positive portrayal of bisexuality in the movies *Sunday, Bloody Sunday* and *Girl Stroke Boy*, but they were rarefied pieces; the world of mainstream entertainment, where rock and roll still operated, had not even seen the arrival on television of camp characters like Mr Humphries and 'Gloria' Beaumont in the sitcoms *Are You Being Served?* and *It Ain't Half Hot, Mum* respectively, or the rise to fame of Larry Grayson. And when those figures did appear, they still hid their sexuality. John Inman, who played Mr Humphries, denied that either he or the character was gay, while in January 1972, at precisely the same time that Bowie was coming out, Grayson was anxious to tell the press: 'I'm not really a queer or a homosexual. I'm just behaving like one. That's the big difference.'[39] But things were to change. Three years later, the television adaptation of Quentin Crisp's autobiography, *The Naked Civil Servant*, would see John Hurt as Crisp concluding that: 'The symbols I adopted forty years ago to express my sexual type have become the uniform of all young people'. By the following decade, homosexuality was part of the mainstream in pop music and television comedy.

arses squeezed into trousers tight at the top and yet baggy all the way down, their shirt collars sticking out of their jacket lapels like glider wings, and homicide in their inkwell eyes.'[32]

The idea of fans dressing up for the occasion was one of the more marked features of the era. 'The glam audience became part of the show,' reflected Mike Leander. 'They dressed up, and it was like a party.'[33] It started with T. Rex, and it soon became established practice for fans to join in by copying the stars on stage, whether it was a striped t-shirt for the Sensational Alex Harvey Band or the feather boas and make-up sported for Roxy Music. 'It was mad,' wrote Noddy Holder of Slade's 1973 gig at Earls Court. 'There were 18,000 people and they were all dressed like Slade. There were loads of top hats with mirrors and silver-clad Dave look-a-likes.'[34] Gary Glitter's fans, being somewhat younger, had to cover their tracks a little: 'A lot of the kids used to arrive with a little suitcase,' he remembered, 'go into the loo, get the gear and put the make-up on and the glitter

Alvin Stardust badge, *c*.1974.
Given by Rob Cooper. V&A: S.1891–2012.

That change in perception was clearly not dependent on Bowie, but during the years of glam he made arguably a larger contribution than anyone else in transforming attitudes. In 1972 it required considerable courage to make a public declaration; it was a leap in the dark, and the fact that his premonitions didn't materialize ('all fucking hell's going to be let loose,' he had feared[40]) has made it seem more straightforward an issue than it really was. It was noticeable that others at a similar stage of their career were disinclined to follow his lead. 'It was a bit of a blow to us when Bowie made it, and the camp thing lost its style and became homosexual,' said Freddie Mercury of Queen the following year, his denial sounding uncannily like that of Larry Grayson. 'It isn't that with us.'[41]

Bowie's public persona provided a sense of validation and identity for those growing up gay in a society where queer-bashing was far from unknown. When a twelve-year-old Boy George spent a day hanging around with other fans in Bowie's garden, he didn't get to see the man himself, but it didn't really matter: 'I met other people like me. I felt like I was part of something.'[42] And in the adult world, Bowie was seen as a positive force within the gay politics of the era, his authenticity vouched for by lyrics that addressed gay sex ('I was stone and he was wax, so he could scream and still relax'[43]), used gay slang ('a trés butch little number'[44]) and spoke of 'a love I could not obey'.[45]

Association with Bowie consequently brought with it a ready-made audience. 'The song made us instant gays; we were tranny magnets when we played the US,' Ian Hunter later said of 'All the Young Dudes'. 'At first I was scared to go into gay bars but it was fabulous, people loved us there.'[46] Initially there was some reluctance to accept this gift horse. 'A lot of people think we're into the campy glitter trip because of our association with David, and we're most definitely not,' Mick Ralphs was at pains to stress. 'I'd just like to say that we're a masculine group.'[47] But a review of a New York gig in 1974 suggested that the band rather came to enjoy the attention: 'Because Hunter camps it up on stage, they attract a similar audience to the New York Dolls: a number of gay young men, glittery dressed young ladies, and general followers of fashion.'[48]

What was perhaps most striking about the sexual politics of glam was the fact that the genre was almost exclusively a male preserve. The audience at a gig by T. Rex or Bowie might be largely female, but the acts on stage very seldom were. There were, of course, attempts made to launch female glam artists: the South African Bobbie McGee's 1973 single 'Rock and Roll People' saw her being tagged 'Gladys Glitter' by the press; Kristine Sparkle (formerly Christine Holmes of 1960s band the Family Dogg) released an album, *Image*, in 1974; Zenda Jacks ('the Goddess of Rock', according to the publicity), brought out the disco-inflected 'Rub My Tummy' the same year; and Linda Beckerman, an operatically trained singer, made her debut with a cover of Chuck Berry's 'Rock 'n' Roll Music', again in 1974, for which she wore 'futuristic, space age, black satin gear, complete with studs, tailcoat, boots and belt'.[49] None of them had a hit. Nor did Ayshea, despite the exposure gained as the presenter of *Lift Off* and the assistance of Roy Wood as writer and producer of her 1973 single 'Farewell'.

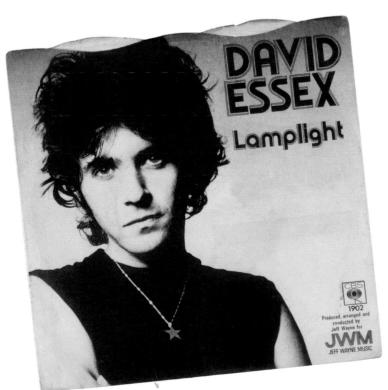

Single sleeve of David Essex, 'Lamplight', 1973.

Not even the involvement of David Bowie in Dana Gillespie's career (another that stretched back to the mid-1960s with an appearance on *Ready Steady Go*) could make her a star with the glam-era *Weren't Born a Man*; both the title track and a version of 'Andy Warhol' missed the charts when released as singles. Bowie had more success with Lulu, with whom he decided to work after a night together in a hotel bedroom in Sheffield following a 1973 gig. A single of 'The Man Who Sold the World' was promoted on television by Lulu in masculine drag, wearing 'a tight-fitting black suit with wide lapels, a black waistcoat, white shirt, a tie and a white fedora hat with a black band, shielding my eyes'.[50] It took the singer in a different direction – curiously dispassionate and virtually immobile, she seemed as though she was commenting on the material rather than living it – and reached number 3 early in 1974, her first top thirty hit since the Eurovision entry 'Boom Bang-a-Bang' back in 1969. It was, however, a one-off, and the projected album with Bowie never happened.

The one great exception was Suzi Quatro, the Detroit-born singer and bassist, who was brought to Britain by producer Mickie Most and who reached number 1 in 1973 with her first hit 'Can the Can' and followed it with '48 Crash', 'Daytona Demon' and 'Devil Gate Drive'. Dressed in black leather, without make-up, and surrounded by a group of male musicians who were considerably larger than her, Quatro was, in her words, 'a very ballsy woman, still feminine but ballsy – knew her own mind, wasn't afraid to speak out, wasn't afraid to tackle the boys at their own game'.[51] She had been gigging in bands since 1964 and was a more than competent musician, which didn't stop male critics from patronizing her. 'That Fender's just too big for a pint-sized chick like you,' ran a live review in the *Melody Maker*. 'It makes you look real cute – and you don't want to be branded with that kind of image, do you?'[52]

Quatro's hits were written by Mike Chapman and Nicky Chinn, the same team who were behind the Sweet and probably the most successful writing partnership since Lennon and McCartney. Indeed in 1974 they were responsible for more singles sales in Britain than the Beatles ever achieved in a calendar year, with further hits coming from Mud and the Arrows, and there was a week that February when they held three of the top four places in the charts. They didn't, however, display the same range of material as the Beatles. 'If you had a formula by which you knew you could sell a million records,' argued Mickie Most, reasonably enough, 'are you going to

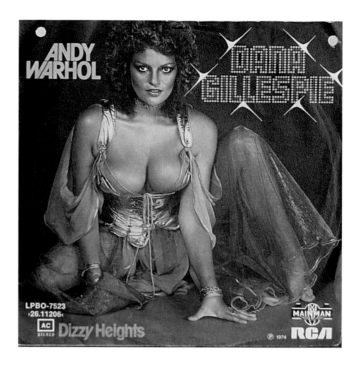

drop it for no reason at all?'[53] So all the records were uptempo, noisy songs that maintained the bubblegum tradition of insistently repetitive choruses and words that sounded right, even if the actual meaning was a little hazy. And all assumed that those too young to vote wanted to have fun. 'We're unfortunately so involved in fighting the bloody government, going on strike,' bemoaned Chapman; 'and the kids, what are they doing? Dancing. And they've got the right idea, they're the happiest people in the country.'[54]

The scale of dominance achieved by Chinnichap (as they were collectively known) led inevitably to suggestions that they were a mere hit factory, handing out material indiscriminately. It was a charge that Quatro was keen to refute: 'Chinn and Chapman tailored whatever they wrote,' she insisted. 'They wrote for me. Mike would listen to me talk, we'd play him a few originals and he'd go away and craft a song for whatever stage we were at.'[55]

There were exceptions. Chinn and Chapman offered the Sweet a new song titled 'Dynamite'; they turned it down, so it went instead to Mud, giving them their first top ten hit. But

German sleeve of Dana Gillespie, 'Andy Warhol', 1973.

Poster of Suzi Quatro, *c*.1974.

SUZI
QUATRO

for the most part, Quatro was quite correct; as the acts developed their own identities – particularly when the bands were allowed to play on their own records – so the songs became increasingly specific. And those identities did tend to come from the bands themselves. 'When we did our live thing, we used to do a little Elvis medley in the middle, and Les [Gray] would do the big Elvis mimic thing,' remembered Rob Davis of Mud. 'Mike Chapman saw this and said, "Oh, we've got to make a record with you sounding like an Elvis impersonator." And that was "Lonely This Christmas".'[56]

Nonetheless, the taint of 'they don't write their own songs' pursued all the Chinnichap acts, damning them in critics' eyes as mere lightweight pop puppets. It was different in America, where Suzi Quatro supported the New York Dolls, and the Sweet appeared with Blue Oyster Cult, but in Britain they struggled to be taken seriously. In vain did the Sweet point to the fact that their producer, Phil Wainman, was also responsible for the Sensational Alex Harvey Band's best album, *Next*, or that both their single 'Blockbuster' and Bowie's 'The Jean Genie' were musically much the same, both having stolen the riff from the Yardbirds' version of 'I'm a Man'. The moment of redemption should have come in 1974, when the Sweet were invited to support the Who at the Valley, Charlton Athletic's stadium in south London, in the company of critically respectable acts like Lou Reed, Bad Company and Humble Pie. 'This might have been the making of the band in a different way in England,' reflected Andy Scott.[57] It wasn't to be; singer Brian Connolly got involved in a fight outside a club, in the course of which he was knocked unconscious and kicked in the throat. The band had to cancel their own tour as well as the stadium gig.

In pursuit of their ambition to be seen as a serious rock band, the Sweet urged Chinnichap to come up with ever heavier material, and weren't reticent about expressing their dissatisfaction in public. 'I don't like our latest record,' Connolly told the press in February 1974, as 'Teenage Rampage' broke into the top three. 'We really believe in our own material at the moment but we've got nothing to offer when it comes to singles commerciality, so we've gone along with Mike and Nicky.'[58] On stage at the Rainbow, Connolly naughtily changed the lyrics of that song from 'imagine the sensation of teenage occupation' to 'imagine the sensation of teenage masturbation',[59] in a show that opened with a stripper and included bassist Steve Priest sucking the tremolo arm of Scott's guitar. 'Theatrics are what the group's into,'

argued Connolly. 'It's not attempting to shock, we do it because musically it's what we're into.'[60]

By the end of 1974, their final Chinnichap single, 'Turn It Down', was banned by *Top of the Pops* for including the lines 'Your old man went and called you a degenerate bum' and 'I can't take no more of that godawful sound so, for God's sake, turn it down'.[61] It was a victory of sorts, claimed Priest: 'We're no longer a teenybopper band who appeal to six-year-olds, we're getting into a more sophisticated bag and have therefore got to prove ourselves to the older kids.'[62]

The Sweet's problems were compounded by the fact that the combination of heavy rock guitars and vocal harmonies was no longer theirs alone. For 1974 also saw the commercial breakthrough of Queen, a band initially dismissed by critics as 'sounding like an ersatz Zeppelin',[63] but now harnessing their heavy metal inclinations to a more disciplined pop sensibility. The key record was the single 'Killer Queen', which reached number 2 in November, just as 'Turn It Down' was failing to make the top forty. 'You almost expect Noël Coward to sing it,' was Freddie Mercury's verdict. 'It's one of those bowler hat, black suspender-belt numbers – not that Noël Coward would wear that.'[64] A tongue-in-cheek piece of vaudeville rock, it was theatrical enough to sound very much like a glam record, though not quite.

'It's about a high-class call girl,' explained Mercury. 'I'm trying to say that classy people can be whores as well.'[65] And perhaps that was the difference. Glam had always concerned itself with the underdog, finding romance in the socially excluded, implicitly accepting the truth of Oscar Wilde's line: 'We are all in the gutter, but some of us are looking at the stars.'[66] Queen appeared to be looking through the other end of the telescope, heading towards the vainglorious declarations of their 1977 hit 'We Are the Champions', with its definitive anti-glam statement: 'No time for losers.'[67] Glam had always had time for losers.

In the meantime, Queen had cornered the rock market in camp, and the Sweet were amongst those who lost out. 'You see, Queen beat us to it,' was Phil Wainman's verdict,[68] and Andy Scott could only agree: 'Queen won the battle. Course they did.'[69]

Freddie Mercury, c.1975.

polydor
STEREO

ST 45

2058 312 A

GUDBUY T' JANE
(Holder - Lea)
SLADE
Produced by Chas Chandler
for Barn Productions

CHANCE MEETING (3.34)
(Ferry)
Produced by BRYAN FERRY and JOHN PUNTER
for E.G. Records Ltd

**BRYAN
FERRY**

WIP.6196-B
WIPX 1323
E.G. Music Ltd
℗ 1974 Island
Records Ltd

ISLAND

RAK
Trade Mark of
RAK RECORDS LTD.

RAK 182
(YRAK.182A) 45

A Mickie Most
Production

Chinnichap/
Rak Publ. Ltd.

Produced by
Mickie Most

**TOUGHEN
UP**
(N. Chinn—
M. Chapman)

ARROWS

℗ 1974
Rak Records
Ltd.

EMI
PUBLIC PERFORMANCE BROADCASTING AND COPYING OF THIS RECORD PROHIBITED·MADE IN GT BRITAIN

ALL ALONE
(Bolan) From LP "Futuristic Dragon"—
BLN 5004

Wizard
Publishing
Ltd.

℗ 1976
Wizard
(Delaware)
Ltd.

Produced by

45 R.P.M.

MARC 16
YMARC 16B

T·REX

MADE IN GREAT BRITAIN

TRADE MARK OF COLUMBIA PICTURES INDUSTRIES INC.
Bell Records Division

bell
Rock Artistes
Mus. Publ. Ltd.

BELL 1368A 45

℗ 1974

BELL 1368

Produced by
Mike Leander
for G.T.O
Prodns.

JUST FOR YOU
(J. Rossall—G. Shephard)

THE GLITTER BAND

In the days of vinyl, and especially before the advent of picture
sleeves for singles, record labels were an important part of the pop
experience. In particular, the RAK and Bell labels, which specialized in
teen pop, established a certain brand loyalty in the early 1970s.

SCIENCE FICTION/ DOUBLE FEATURE

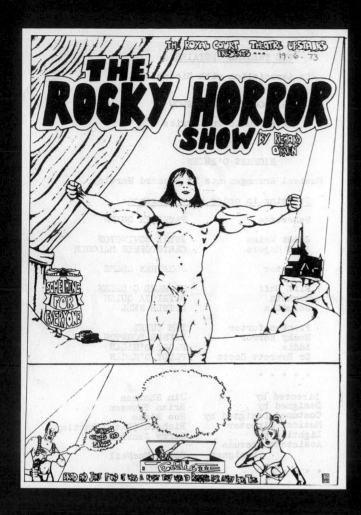

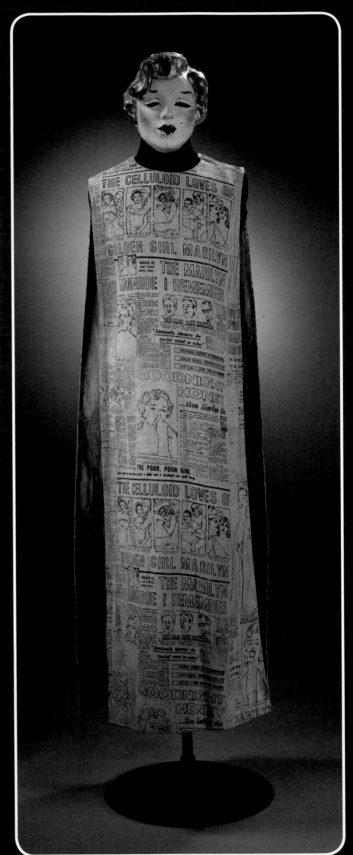

008-603

Roger Daltrey in *Lisztomania*, 1975.

MARC

6

TUMBLING DOWN

A TRIBUTE IN WORDS AND PICTURES TO

MARC BOLAN

40p

The Boy Who Was Born To Boogie

We were dressed in our snazziest gear with flared trousers and all that, and there's all these punks there with drainpipe jeans.

John Springate, The Glitter Band

Poster magazine to mark the death of Marc Bolan, 1977.
Published by Associated Magazine Distributors.

As the three-day week was starting in January 1974, David Bowie gave an interview to the *Melody Maker*, with the paper reporting: 'David feels that politics are going to play a much bigger part in rock music this year, and says it only needs one figurehead to emerge who could take over.'[1] He had at the time just been rebuffed by George Orwell's widow, Sonia, in his attempt to adapt *Nineteen Eighty-Four* as a stage musical, and the idea that the political, economic and social crises of the decade were heading towards a totalitarian solution was evidently much in his mind.

With the collapse of the projected musical, Bowie reworked those songs he'd already written into an album, *Diamond Dogs*, that made his point more effectively than a straight adaptation of Orwell could ever have achieved. In the absence of Mick Ronson and Ken Scott, the arrangements and the textures of the music were darker, denser and more claustrophobic than anything Bowie, or any other rock artist, had previously released. The fragmented words that emerged from the murky depths of the mix (unusually for Bowie, it didn't come with a lyric sheet) suggested the desperation of a man trying to keep a grip on humanity in a world that was crumbling; on the first side in particular – a collection of songs that didn't resolve themselves but petered out in chaos, blended into the next track or were abruptly conjoined – it seemed as though the collapse of society that he was depicting was also destroying the precision and perfectionism of glam itself.

It was a magnificently ambitious album that captured the paranoid tenor of the times, and if some of it came to sound absurdly melodramatic with its talk of a city overrun by 'rats the size of cats',[2] that too suited the Britain of the first half of the 1970s, where normal life struggled to continue amidst power cuts and social decay. 'In some places the piles of rotting garbage rise as high as twenty feet,' reported the press,[3] as the army was sent in to deal with the effects of a refuse workers' strike in Glasgow. 'The biggest hazard the soldiers face is the swarms of rats at every temporary rubbish dump.'[4] On a wider scale, the election of Harold Wilson had, for many, seemed like a caving in to trade union power, and there were those who felt that the political system itself had failed. 'Two years ago we could have easily faced a coup in Britain,' wrote the union leader Jack Jones in 1977. 'The fear of hyper-inflation was strong. There was talk of private armies being assembled. There was talk of the end of democracy.'[5] It was, declared Bowie, 'the year of the scavenger, the season of the bitch'.[6]

The album went to number 1 in Britain (dislodging the Carpenters' rather more reassuring *The Singles 1969–73*) and became his first top ten hit in America, where it was promoted with a tour that started in June 1974. It was an unprecedented show, the closest that rock music had come to a full Broadway experience, with a huge set that placed the band firmly off to the side, leaving the stage clear for the star and his accompanying dancers to act out the songs in a spectacle that involved no interaction at all with the audience. It was a 'completely rehearsed and choreographed routine where every step and nuance has been perfected down to the last detail'. complained critics. 'There isn't one iota of spontaneity.'[7]

It was as though Bowie were trying to reinvoke the discipline and control that had marked his work up until *Diamond Dogs*.

He himself appeared in a new guise, dressed in a sharp but conservative powder-blue suit with red braces, though for audiences that included a large number of Ziggy and Aladdin Sane clones, he remained satisfyingly alien, now cadaverous even by his standards and clearly showing the effects of what was fast becoming a ferocious cocaine habit. Reflecting later on the cover of the resultant album, *David Live*, he reached for a Jacques Brel allusion: 'That cover – my God – it looks as if I've just stepped out of the grave, and that's basically how I felt. The record should have been called *David Bowie Is Alive and Well and Living Only in Theory*.'[8]

The live album itself was lacklustre, with uninspired musical performances by a band that had been in dispute with Bowie himself over payments for the recording, almost up to the moment of the show starting. Appropriately for a time when militant trade unionism and economic mismanagement were being referred to, even in the *Wall Street Journal*, as 'the British disease',[9] it was the two British musicians in the band, bassist Herbie Flowers and drummer Tony Newman, who acted in the capacity of shop stewards, leading the demand for a bonus payment.

The same situation had arisen the previous year when their predecessors, Trevor Bolder and Woody Woodmansey, had discovered that their wages were considerably lower than the newly recruited American pianist, Mike Garson. Some of this was simply the result of MainMan, Bowie's management company, looking after the pennies even as the pounds were being poured away in the most profligate manner possible, but there was also an inherent conflict between the star's self-celebration and his dependence on a band. 'It was Ziggy and the Spiders until it became really big,' remembered Woodmansey, 'then it became Bowie and somebody else in the background.'[10]

This had long been an issue in rock and roll – it was, after all, the basic narrative of *Stardust* – but it seemed particularly problematic in glam, since the genre had placed such an emphasis on a shared fantasy in the first place. 'You're the blessed, we're the Spiders from Mars,' Bowie had sung,[11] and the first half of that formulation, sanctifying the fans, had been central to glam's appeal. Cockney Rebel ended their gigs with 'Tumbling Down', a song that closed on a dramatic singalong chorus of 'Oh dear, look what they've done to the blues',[12] during which Harley would leave the crowd to finish on their own: 'At the end when I leave the audience singing and walk off stage, I'm saying you don't need me anymore,' he explained.[13] But the shared experience was falling apart; Mott the Hoople and Slade were finding that success was distancing them from their working-class roots, and it was increasingly evident that glam was not characterized by any concept of democracy within groups. Roxy Music had found that when Bryan Ferry unilaterally decided to bring in Eddie Jobson to replace Eno, while Marc Bolan had never even pretended that T. Rex was any kind of partnership of equals, keeping the other members of the band on low wages throughout the glory years.

A similar problem arose with Cockney Rebel, who completed a triumphant British tour to promote their second album, *The Psychomodo*, in July 1974 and promptly split, with Milton Reame-James reported in the music press to be unhappy that his contributions to tracks like 'Sebastian' and 'Tumbling Down' received no credit. Steve Harley professed

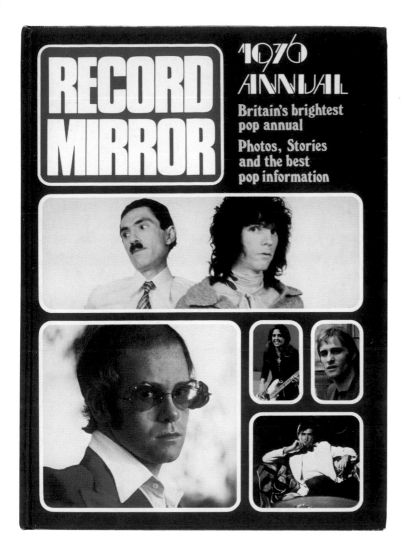

('Art is not a pastime, but a priesthood'). Much of the music on that record, including its accompanying single, 'Jet Silver and the Dolls of Venus', had inevitably attracted comparisons with Bowie, an association that the group's leader, Bill Nelson, was keen to play down. 'I see that as primarily because of our similar backgrounds,' he explained. 'I was doing multi-media things at art college and into very similar areas of literature and music – so you're bound to get things coming out at a similar level.'[15] Nonetheless, following a final headlining gig at Biba, Nelson broke up the band, reforming with a new, though temporary, line-up including Reame-James and bassist Paul Jeffreys from Cockney Rebel. Subsequent releases veered away from any glam comparisons.

In America too, groups were reaching the end of the line. The original band trading under the name Alice Cooper had recorded seven albums together, but during the course of 1974 the singer decided it was time for a change: 'I realized that I couldn't go on doing the same kind of thing with the Alice character. It was develop or destroy him.'[16] By the time of his next album, *Welcome to My Nightmare*, again released as Alice Cooper, he had shed the rest of the group, effectively appropriating the name and the act for himself.

Newer acts struggled even more. Jobriath's second album, *Creatures of the Street*, disappeared almost without trace and, during his first national tour, he was dropped by both his record label and his manager, subsequently opting out of rock altogether. Also having their record deal cancelled were the New York Dolls, whose second album, *Too Much Too Soon*, failed to provide a breakthrough, despite being produced by the legendary Shangri-Las producer George 'Shadow' Morton (he had earlier been responsible for Mott the Hoople's 'Midnight Lady' single). As their drug use escalated, there was a feeling that the Dolls were, in the words of one live review, 'hooked to a time that's inexorably rolling away'.[17] Or, possibly, that they were simply ahead of their time, as journalist Chris Charlesworth predicted: 'Perhaps in five years time, their albums will be hailed as works of art and David Johansen, Johnny Thunders and Co. will be

himself entirely unconcerned at the mutiny. 'I don't care if you think of me as a big-headed little bastard,' he told the press; 'I believe I could go out and have four cardboard cut-outs and a tape machine and I'd still get the same reception, the same reaction.'[14] Retaining only drummer Stuart Elliott, he formed another incarnation of the band, Steve Harley and Cockney Rebel, to make sure that credit went where he felt it was due. He went on to score his biggest hit with the number 1 single 'Make Me Smile (Come Up and See Me)' – a song about the break-up of the original band – but thereafter his music lacked the imaginative arrangements that had brought him success, and he was never again to match the inspired beauty of those first two albums.

Supporting Cockney Rebel on that tour were a new band, Be-Bop Deluxe, whose debut album, *Axe Victim*, had featured on the back of the sleeve a photo of them wearing heavy make-up, under a quote from Jean Cocteau: '*Ne plus envisager l'art commune une distraction, mais comme un sacerdoce*' resurrected in much the same way as Lou Reed has made his recent comeback.'[18]

The immediate future in America belonged to groups that took elements of glam and attached them to a more mainstream appeal. Aerosmith came from Boston but were signed while playing in New York, where their slightly sleazy take on rock and roll clearly had a precedent. 'I was in awe of the Dolls,' admitted singer Steven Tyler. 'They used to say I was a Jagger lookalike, but Johansen had lips for miles.'[19] The onstage relationship between Tyler and guitarist Joe Perry was clearly based on that of David Johansen and Johnny Thunders, even if that was itself based on Mick Jagger and Keith Richards.

There was also Kiss, a New York band with all the right attitudes. They had come together when Gene Simmons contacted Peter Criss in response to a small ad. 'Before I asked him about his musical ideas, I asked whether he was fat, if he wore a beard and things like that,' recounted Criss. 'We had to get the visuals right from the start.'[20] They began by wearing make-up in the style of the New York Dolls, but soon began to veer closer to that of Alice Cooper and Zal Cleminson: a comic-book image that completely obscured their features. 'Some people will do anything to get attention,' remarked an amused Alice Cooper, adding ironically: 'They're good, but what they need is a gimmick.' They also had the right source material. 'Slade were certainly our greatest

influence, not only in the drafting of rock songs, but also as performers,' acknowledged Simmons.[21] Fun though it all was, there was no mystique or glamour about the band, and the music was essentially a bubblegum heavy metal, closer to the Sweet than to Roxy Music. They became huge in America.

Roxy themselves were not immune to the growing sense of an era coming to a close. 'I mean, the band will split, inevitably – it's that sort of band,' shrugged Eddie Jobson. 'I'll give it till Bryan is as big in America as he is here, then he'll leave and the group will disband. Everybody knows that.'[22] In the meantime Roxy seemed to share Bowie's premonitions of a totalitarian future. Their British tour in the autumn of 1974 saw Bryan Ferry wearing padded shoulders, riding breeches and boots, while the shows attracted comments about Nuremburg rallies. ACHTUNG ROXY ran the headline to the *Melody Maker*'s review of their performance at the Rainbow, suggesting that the set 'wouldn't have seemed out of place in some grotesque Nazi epic like *Triumph of the Will*, or alternatively would have graced the fall of the Hapsburg Empire'.[23] Ferry subsequently made it clear which of those alternatives he had had in mind: 'The Nazis had a great sense of visuals. What we were doing with all that theatre was to create a style which matched the music.'[24]

At the poppier end of the market, there was still a determination not to get sidetracked by socio-political issues. 'Rock really must have more to do with fantasy than reality,' insisted Gary Glitter,[25] holding on to the creed that brought him a third number 1 single in 1974 with 'Always Yours'. He too, though, had some problems with his backing group who, under the name of the Glitter Band, began playing their own gigs and, in March 1974, made their debut single, 'Angel Face'. Released at the same time as Glitter's new single, 'Remember Me This Way', it spent longer in the top ten and sold more copies than did their master's voice; in the future, Glitter's management would ensure that the two acts had their releases carefully separated, so as to avoid any further harm to his ego.

Bubblegum manufactured to tie in with Kiss' album
Unmasked **(1980).**

(opposite)
Sleeve of the Glitter Band's *Hey!* (Bell, 1974).

'If there is hope,' observed Winston Smith in *Nineteen Eighty-Four*, 'it lies in the proles.'[26] In a similar way, glam had at its peak held to the populist celebration of mass taste, but increasingly those with higher artistic aspirations were feeling wary of being tainted by the pop acts who had come under the same umbrella. By late 1974 it was only Eno who continued to celebrate the values of pop, arguing that acts like the Sweet and Alvin Stardust were 'taking a certain number of new elements from progressive music and merging them in with melody and good production and from that making pop hit records. They're the ones who're making the real new sounds.'[27] He also recognized that Mike Leander and Chinn and Chapman were 'doing something very interesting. Certainly as important as Phil Spector was to the Sixties.' It was an attitude with which at least some of the pop acts would agree. 'I love pop, I think it's instant and it hits hard,'

The Sweet

流行音樂
Popular musical entertainment

Book now
Some tickets still available
at Box Office, City Hall
尚餘部份門券
在大會堂售票處或售詢即訂座

Concert poster from The Sweet's Japanese tour, 1976.
V&A: S.4712–1995.

(Opposite)
Fashion spread from *Petticoat* magazine showing the impact
of retro styles on the high street, October 1973.

said Mud's Dave Mount. 'Pop isn't meant to last, it's here today and gone tomorrow.'[28] Or, as Mike Chapman liked to say: 'There ain't no crap, there ain't no chaff in Chinn and Chap.'[29]

But even the Chinnichap hit machine was running into problems. Following 'Turn It Down', the Sweet decided they could write their own material and, with 'Fox on the Run' in early 1975, scored their biggest hit for nearly two years. Mud followed them in leaving the stable, while Suzi Quatro struggled to maintain her run of hits. A new act was added, in the form of Smokey – swiftly renamed Smokie after complaints from Motown about possible confusion with Smokey Robinson – but they were very definitely pitched as a non-glam group, even though they had served as Peter Noone's backing band at the time of his cover of 'Oh You Pretty Things'. 'They were looking for a band they could promote more as an album band and less bubblegum pop,' remembered singer Chris Norman.[30] Their first album, *Pass It Around*, mostly comprised original material, and they became the first Chinnichap act to be invited onto *The Old Grey Whistle Test*.

'From 1974 on, a lot changed, not only for us but for all the other glam bands,' reflected Noddy Holder in his autobiography. 'The scene had become so big so fast that the bubble had to burst. There was nowhere else glam could go. The outfits couldn't get any more outrageous and the records couldn't get any rowdier.'[31] Marc Bolan, whose records were suffering from a very marked drop in quality – 'So long Marc, it's been good to know you,' read one review of 'Light of Love' in 1974[32] – was later to claim that he shared the public's growing wish for change: 'The glam rock thing was alright for the early '70s, but by 1974 I was just bored.'[33]

In fact, Bolan had been expressing his dissatisfaction with stardom in interviews as early as 1972. 'I've worked eight years for what I've got now, but in the end I don't know what it's worth, how I'm gonna come out of the whole thing.'[34] Others shared his distaste. 'The idea of being screamed at by little girls – it made my skin crawl,' said Jim Lea; 'I was very psychologically disturbed by it.'[35] There was also a dawning recognition, as in every cycle of pop music, that the demands of the industry were ultimately dehumanizing. 'He's not so much a person as a puppet,' the trailer for *Privilege* had trumpeted, and the same imagery turned up in *Stardust*. 'I thought you were not like the others,' Jim Maclaine's girlfriend tells him. 'You are not a marionette.' And that too was the subject of Mott the Hoople's song 'Marionette'. This was the flip side to stardom,

and the wearying effects of the treadmill were becoming apparent as the fantasy faltered.

But although an end was probably in sight for glam anyway, its arrival was hastened by the industrial conflicts that it tried so hard to ignore. A strike by technicians at the BBC meant that *Top of the Pops* was not aired for over a month in the early summer of 1974, with a major impact on those acts who relied on the television exposure. 'The marketing shifted,' remembered John Springate of the Glitter Band. 'What happened was people weren't hearing records on *Top of the Pops*, they were hearing them in discos, so suddenly disco started coming through a little bit more than usual.'[36]

The charts in July and August were indeed dominated by the sounds of disco and by the sweet soul coming out of Philadelphia, with records including George McCrae's 'Rock Your Baby', the Three Degrees' 'When Will I See You Again' and the Stylistics' 'You Make Me Feel Brand New'. In September 1974 Barry White had his first top ten single in Britain, fifteen months after his debut hit, and by December he was at number 1 with 'You're the First, the Last, My

Everything'. Also scoring their debut top ten single were KC and the Sunshine Band ('Queen of Clubs'), while the number 1 hits included Carl Douglas's 'Kung Fu Fighting', Sweet Sensation's 'Sad Sweet Dreamer' and Ken Boothe's 'Everything I Own', the latter being the first reggae record to top the charts since Dave and Ansil Collins's 'Double Barrel' more than three years earlier, before the glam deluge.

In the process, some hitherto reliable hit-makers found that the charts could no longer be taken for granted. Suzi Quatro's 'Too Big' failed to make the top ten, Wizzard's 'This Is the Story of My Love (Baby)' missed the top thirty after five consecutive top ten hits, and so too did David Essex's 'America', the only one of his first seven singles not to make the top ten. (The latter did extremely good business in France, however, where the stuttering chorus – 'America-ca-ca-uh-huh' – sounded like he was using the slang word 'caca' to describe the leading nation of the Western world.) It was not a good time to be launching a new act, as the vocal trio Thunderthighs discovered; having provided backing vocals on everything from Lou Reed's 'Walk on the Wild Side' to

(Left)
Brett Smiley appears on *Russell Harty Plus* (ITV, 1974).

(Bottom)
Poster advertising Mick Ronson's solo album
***Slaughter on 10th Avenue*, 1974.**

(Opposite)
***Words* magazine, featuring Mick Ronson, 1974.**

Mott the Hoople's 'Roll Away the Stone', they released their debut single, 'Central Park Arrest', in June 1974, only to see it stall at number 30.

As Paul Gambaccini wrote that September: 'The tra la days of glitter rock are over.'[37] A month later the same writer concluded: 'The overnight demise of glam rock ties in too comfortably with the disappearance of *Top of the Pops* from the nation's screens to be mere coincidence. Soul has filled the vacuum.'[38]

The change in taste was illustrated by the fortunes of Brett Smiley, an eighteen-year-old American singer who should have been a guaranteed success. Beautiful and talented, he was the protégé of former Rolling Stones manager Andrew Loog Oldham, and made his British television debut on Russell Harty's popular chat show singing 'Space Ace', the b-side to his debut single 'Va Va Va Voom'. The record was promoted with full-page adverts in the music press, and he even got the front page of *Disc*. But this was September 1974, and he was a year too late. The single made no impact at all, and the album he'd recorded had to wait three decades before being released to coincide with Nina Antonia's memoir, *The Prettiest Star: Whatever Happened to Brett Smiley?*

Around the same time, on the other side of the world, a group called Space Waltz were making their television debut, singing 'Out On The Street' on the New Zealand version of

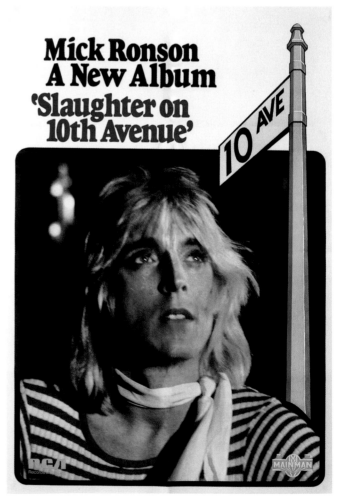

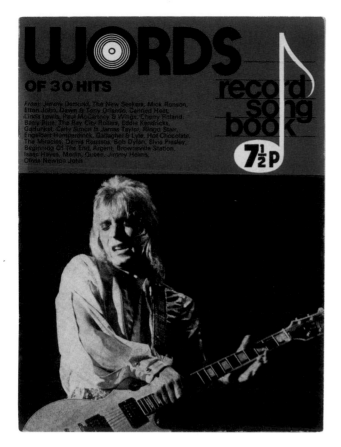

New Faces. A vehicle for the songs of vocalist Alastair Riddell, Space Waltz did release an album, full of swooning Bowie-esque epics, much of it based on an invented mythology about 'a genetically engineered race from the planet Telluria, whose inhabitants use sex purely as a reproductive process where no love is involved'.[39] Again, though, it was to be thirty years before it was released outside New Zealand.

The blacking out of *Top of the Pops* also affected Mott the Hoople. Their new single, 'Foxy Foxy', didn't reach the top thirty, making the strategy of going for hit singles look a little precarious. A revival of fortunes was hoped for, however, with the recruitment in the autumn of Mick Ronson as the group's guitarist. Ronson had been looking a little lost since his split with Bowie a year earlier, despite being launched as a solo act at the beginning of the year with a flourish and a fanfare. His debut album, *Slaughter on 10th Avenue*, and single, a cover of 'Love Me Tender', had been accompanied by a solo tour that opened at the Rainbow. None of it was entirely convincing. His singing wasn't strong enough and he lacked the arrogant self-confidence to be a front man, as the live reviews sadly concluded: 'He wasn't ready for this big hype and he couldn't sustain it.'[40] The first album got through the critics on

goodwill, for everyone liked him – even Lou Reed, not always noted for his lavish distribution of praise, said he was 'a lovely man'[41] – and it reached the top ten but, just like Jobriath, the hype caught up with him on his second album, and he gracefully and gratefully bowed out of the limelight.

His union with Mott should have been a match made in glam heaven, but it didn't work out. Ronson was still being managed by MainMan, an organization whose lavish extravagance, funded by Bowie's record sales, meant that its artists were treated like royalty. 'I was used to eating beans on toast and fish fingers,' remembered Overend Watts, marvelling at the fact that when he went to Ronson's flat, 'it was all caviar in the fridge and champagne everywhere.'[42] The disparity continued when the group went on a European tour; two limousines turned up at the airport, one for the band and a bigger one for the guitarist.

From the outside, such issues meant little compared to the single that emerged from the new line-up. 'Saturday Gigs' was perhaps the best thing the group had ever recorded, a funny, melancholy song that took Mott's tendency towards self-documentation to its final point, recounting the history of the group from 1969 and wrapping it in an epic production. It couldn't help but feel like a farewell from the band and from glam, particularly when the words of Ian Hunter's closing rap were deciphered beneath the storm of the fade-out: 'Don't you ever forget us, we'll never forget you,' he called out. 'So long for now.'[43] It was their least successful single in over three years, missing out on the top forty, and just before Christmas 1974 the group announced that it was splitting up.

The other great people's band were also feeling the winds of change. Slade's film *Flame* was released in January 1975, preceded by its soundtrack album and a single 'Far, Far Away'. In retrospect the movie has been acclaimed as one of the better pieces of 1970s British film-making, but at the time its grubby, violent depiction of a cynical music industry – it had to be re-edited to avoid an 'X' certificate – didn't really satisfy the group's existing fans and certainly didn't win them any new ones. It was intended as a mark of a maturing group, a response to growing criticism that they weren't progressing. 'People used to say: you've had all these hits like the Beatles did, when are you going to do *Sgt Pepper*?' remembered Dave Hill. 'Unfortunately we didn't have any songs about pilchards climbing up the Eiffel Tower.'[44] They did, however, have the epic, piano- and brass-dominated 'How Does It Feel?', which accompanied the film's title sequence; released as a single, it broke their run of twelve consecutive top ten hits.

Badge for Slade's film *Flame*, 1975.

Given by Rob Cooper. V&A: S.1896–2012.

Further straws in the wind at the end of 1974 came with the departure of saxophonist John Rossall from the Glitter Band, the group that he had formed to back Gary Glitter. Silverhead split up after appearing in October at the Hollywood Palladium alongside the New York Dolls and Iggy and the Stooges in a gig that was billed as 'The Death of Glitter'. And, in a truly symbolic gesture, Eno had his hair cut short.

But if there was a single moment that signified the end of glam, it was the release in September 1974 of David Bowie's new single, a cover of the soul standard 'Knock On Wood'. It wasn't a very impressive version, but the choice of material spoke volumes. 'It's one hell of a departure,' noted the *Record Mirror*.[45] Bowie, it appeared, had lost interest in rock and roll and fallen under the spell of the new soul sounds on the Philadelphia International label, where Kenny Gamble and Leon Huff wrote and produced hits for Billy Paul, the O'Jays and Harold Melvin and the Blue Notes (in effect, running a stable just like Chinn and Chapman). By October, the Diamond

Dogs tour had mutated completely, with the jettisoning of the elaborate set and its replacement by a straightforward band on stage, fronted by Bowie, delivering a soul set. The ensuing album, *Young Americans*, was a radical break with everything he had previously done and yielded his first American number 1 with 'Fame'.

Roxy Music were soon to be found making a similar journey. Prefaced by Bryan Ferry's Philly-style reworking of the 1930s classic 'You Go to My Head', they released 'Love Is the Drug' in 1975. 'I suppose it's sort of a disco record,' suggested Ferry, which was understating the case a little; it was tailor-made for the dance floor. Others too began to explore this new territory: clavinet riffs turned up on Slade's 'Thanks for the Memory' and on Suzi Quatro's 'Your Mama Won't Like Me'; 'Dreamy Lady' was released by the rebranded T. Rex Disco Party; 'New York Groove' by a young Mike Leander-produced band, Hello, sounded like a Hamilton Bohannon track; and the Glitter Band put funk instrumentals 'Makes You Blind' and 'Tuna Biscuit' on their b-sides.

Disco shared with glam a taste for hedonism, for escapism in the face of economic crisis, as well as its rejection of blues-rock jamming and its acceptance of homosexuality and of those marginalized by society. It was no great surprise when Sylvester reinvented himself as the self-proclaimed Queen of Disco. There was, however, a marked difference in the way the critics and the public took to the various manifestations of disco's takeover from glam. The work of Bowie and Roxy was accepted as legitimate artistic development; that of the others tended to be dismissed as bandwagon-jumping at best, and more often as a sign of desperation.

Meanwhile, in case there was any doubt that glam (and possibly music itself) had come to the end of the road, Lou Reed, who had once written such pretty, if perverse, pop songs, created *Metal Machine Music*, an hour-long instrumental piece comprising multiple guitars feeding back on themselves in an aural onslaught that studiously avoided melody, harmony and rhythm. In a stroke of malevolent genius that was almost literally beyond belief, Reed persuaded RCA Records not only to release the piece as a double album, but also to issue a quadraphonic version. Allegedly the record sold 100,000 copies in America.

The days of peacock preening were clearly on the wane. At its peak, glam had kept the nation's youth supplied with beauty and danger, fantasy and fun. But its time had passed. The charts now were full of American disco and of British groups recreating the high school pop of the Kennedy years: the Bay City Rollers, Rubettes and Showaddywaddy. Where glam had used early rock and roll as a launch pad into the unknown, this was unthreatening revivalism, more Marty Wilde than Oscar.

Even so, the dying echoes of glam could still be heard in 1975. The Sensational Alex Harvey Band began to achieve the record sales that had previously eluded them, while Sparks became even odder on their fifth album, *Indiscreet*. There was the success of Fox, whose singer Noosha came across like a more commercial Dagmar Krause from Slapp Happy, and the year ended with Sailor's first hit, 'Glass of Champagne', making its way up the charts where it reached number 2, kept from the top place only by Queen's 'Bohemian Rhapsody'.

There was also the emergence on the live scene of the Doctors of Madness, with a show 'loosely structured to convey a narrative of a guy having a nervous breakdown onstage'.[46] Their debut album, *Late Night Movies, All Night Brainstorms*, released in 1976, sounded like the missing link between *The Human Menagerie* and *Diamond Dogs*, with the

violin and mannered vocals of the former and the melodrama of the latter. 'They reflect in the '70s the decadence of Berlin in the '30s,' proclaimed their manager, Justin de Villeneuve,[47] though that made them sound more derivative than they were. The album's climactic closing track, the fifteen-minute 'Mainlines', opened in histrionic fashion ('This is the place the rats come to die') and ended on a classic descending-note glam riff, as the band's blue-haired singer, Kid Strange, called out in desperation: 'Mainline trains could never find drivers to run a service out to here.'[48] They were the last of the great glam bands. Or possibly they were the first of the great punk bands.

Poster for the Sensational Alex Harvey's Band's first compilation album, *Big Hits and Close Shaves*, 1977.

(above)
Concert poster for Sailor, 1976.
V&A: S.4374–1995.

'Someone's got to come along and say: Fuck you,' Alex Harvey had warned in 1973, as he bemoaned the state of modern rock.[49] He returned to the theme the following year: 'I tell you, some time soon a dirty rotten little band will come along and change everything.'[50] And sure enough, in 1976, John Springate and Gerry Shephard of the Glitter Band went to see a much talked-about new group called the Sex Pistols. 'Gerry and I were dressed in our snazziest gear with flared trousers and all that, and there's all these punks there with drainpipe jeans, short hair, really sort of "now",' recalled Springate. 'The Sex Pistols came on and did four numbers and I said to Gerry: Well that's it then.'[51]

Punk, of course, was largely populated by those who had grown up on glam, whether as musicians – Joey of the Ramones was formerly Jeffrey Hyman of New York glam band, Sniper – or as fans – Johnny Rotten's audition for the Pistols consisted of him singing along to Alice Cooper's 'Eighteen'. The vast majority of British punks had grown up with T. Rex, the Spiders from Mars and Mott the Hoople, and most were quick to claim the Stooges and the New York Dolls as well. The influence could be seen in the cover versions: Siouxsie and the Banshees' '20th Century Boy', the Skids' 'All the Young Dudes' and Eater's 'Fifteen' (an age-adjusted remake of 'Eighteen'). For despite the superficial differences, punk – like disco – had much in common with glam: there were art school backgrounds, references to Weimar and science fiction, a love of the seven-inch single and of invented names, a taste for provocation and for excessive dressing up ('I did like some of the clothes,' approved Dave Hill[52]).

The first of the glam stars to respond to the challenge of punk was Marc Bolan, who had long since fallen from commercial favour – he hadn't had a top ten single since July 1973 – but who was still fondly regarded by many. At the beginning of 1977 he toured the country with punk band the Damned as his support act, and his new album, *Dandy in the Underworld*, stripped down his sound and regained something of the old swagger. Later that year he was given an afternoon television show, attracting an audience of up to ten million, on which he provided a platform for some of the leading punk groups. Amongst them were Generation X, who appeared on the final episode. Also on that show was David Bowie, promoting his new single 'Heroes' and joining Bolan for what was supposed to be a duet, the first time that the two founders of glam had worked together since Bolan had played on Bowie's single 'The Prettiest Star', recorded in January 1970.

Present for the occasion was another glam veteran, Phil Wainman, producer of the Sweet and the Sensational Alex Harvey Band, who was now working with Generation X on their new single, 'Wild Youth'. No great fan of the band, he found himself becoming increasingly angered as the rehearsal time came and went without the group having even arrived. By the time they did turn up, shortly before recording was due to start, the schedule had been sufficiently thrown out that it started fifteen minutes late, a potentially disastrous delay at a time when television studios were dominated by stringent union practices. ('You weren't even allowed to plug your own guitar amp into the mains socket, or adjust a microphone to your height,' was Tony Visconti's memory of the era. 'Any transgression of the rules threatened a union walkout.'[53])

And so it was that the final duet was abruptly terminated before a word could be sung. 'The bloody lights went out,' recalled Wainman. 'They were very unionized at Granada and they pulled the bloody plug. Everything went out. The band kept playing, but they played out in the dark. The climax of the show was there for a minute and then gone for the next two minutes. And that was because Generation X turned up late. And I just think that's despicable. Despicable.'[54] The great glam summit of Bowie and Bolan had fallen victim to a combination of punk attitude and trade union regulations.

It was Bolan's last recording. A week later, on 16 September 1977, he was killed in a car crash in Barnes, London. The headline on the front page of the *Record Mirror* simply read: GLAM ROCK IS DEAD.

Sleeve of T. Rex single, 'Dandy in the Underworld', 1977.

AFTER ALL

CHRONOLOGY

SINGLES

David Bowie, 'The Prettiest Star'
Kinks, 'Lola'
Mungo Jerry, 'In the Summertime'
Alice Cooper, 'Eighteen'
T. Rex, 'Ride a White Swan'
Dave Edmunds, 'I Hear You Knocking'

T. Rex, 'Hot Love'
Slade, 'Get Down and Get With It'
Mott the Hoople, 'Midnight Lady'
Alice Cooper, 'Under My Wheels'
T. Rex, 'Get It On'
Slade, 'Coz I Luv You'

David Bowie, 'Changes'
T. Rex, 'Telegram Sam'
T. Rex, 'Metal Guru'
Slade, 'Take Me Bak 'Ome'
Gary Glitter, 'Rock and Roll (Part Two)'
David Bowie, 'Starman'
Alice Cooper, 'School's Out'
Mott the Hoople, 'All the Young Dudes'
Roxy Music, 'Virginia Plain'
Slade, 'Mama Weer All Crazee Now'
Sweet, 'Wig-Wam Bam'
T. Rex, 'Children of the Revolution'
Kinks, 'Celluloid Heroes'
David Bowie, 'John I'm Only Dancing'
Alice Cooper, 'Elected'
Elton John, 'Crocodile Rock'
Slade, 'Gudbuy t'Jane'
David Bowie, 'The Jean Genie'
Wizzard, 'Ball Park Incident'

1970   1971   1972

ALBUMS

Tyrannosaurus Rex, *A Beard of Stars*
Alice Cooper, *Easy Action*
Stooges, *Fun House*
Velvet Underground, *Loaded*
Mott the Hoople, *Mad Shadows*
Slade, *Play It Loud*
David Bowie, *The Man Who Sold the World*
T. Rex, *T. Rex*

Alice Cooper, *Love It to Death*
T. Rex, *Electric Warrior*
Halfnelson (aka Sparks), *Halfnelson*
Mott the Hoople, *Brain Capers*
Alice Cooper, *Killer*
David Bowie, *Hunky Dory*

Slade, *Slade Alive*
Lou Reed, *Lou Reed*
Sparks, *A Woofer in Tweeter's Clothing*
Alice Cooper, *School's Out*
David Bowie, *Ziggy Stardust*
Roxy Music, *Roxy Music*
T. Rex, *The Slider*
Mott the Hoople, *All the Young Dudes*
Bette Midler, *The Divine Miss M*
Slade, *Slayed?*
Lou Reed, *Transformer*

CULTURE

Beatles split
Deaths of Jimi Hendrix and Janis Joplin
Performance (film)
Woodstock (film)
Oh Calcutta! (London stage)
Sounds becomes Britain's fifth weekly rock paper

Death of Jim Morrison
Death in Venice (film)
The Devils (film)
Sunday, Bloody Sunday (film)
Girl Stroke Boy (film)
The Boy Friend (film)
The Last Picture Show (film)
The Old Grey Whistle Test starts on television
Pork (London stage)
Godspell (London stage)
Let It Rock (shop) opens

A Clockwork Orange (film)
Cabaret (film)
Savage Messiah (film)
Jesus Christ Superstar (London stage)
The Threepenny Opera (London stage)
The Good Old Bad Old Days (London stage)
Tutankhamen exhibition (London)
Wembley Rock and Roll Show

EVENTS

Edward Heath elected prime minister
British voting age reduced from 21 to 18

Decimal currency introduced
Charles Manson and followers convicted of
conspiracy to murder
Joe Frazier beats Muhammad Ali to retain
world heavyweight title

Miners' strike
Bloody Sunday killings in Londonderry
First Gay Pride march in Britain
Richard Nixon re-elected US president

Column 1973 (singles):

Sweet, 'Blockbuster'
Alice Cooper, 'Hello Hurray'
Slade, 'Cum On Feel the Noize'
T. Rex, '20th Century Boy'
Roxy Music, 'Pyjamarama'
Mud, 'Crazy'
Suzi Quatro, 'Can the Can'
David Bowie, 'Drive-In Saturday'
Alice Cooper, 'No More Mr Nice Guy'
Wizzard, 'See My Baby Jive'
Lou Reed, 'Walk on the Wild Side'
Mott the Hoople, 'Honaloochie Boogie'
Gary Glitter, 'I'm the Leader of the Gang'
David Essex, 'Rock On'
Sensational Alex Harvey Band, 'Giddy Up a Ding Dong'
Mott the Hoople, 'All the Way from Memphis'
Sweet, 'Ballroom Blitz'
Bryan Ferry, 'A Hard Rain's Gonna Fall'
David Bowie, 'Sorrow'
Sensational Alex Harvey Band, 'The Faith Healer'
Alvin Stardust, 'My Coo-Ca-Choo'
Roxy Music, 'Street Life'
Mott the Hoople, 'Roll Away the Stone'
Jobriath, 'Earthling'
Wizzard, 'I Wish It Could Be Christmas Everyday'
Slade, 'Merry Xmas Everybody'
Leo Sayer, 'The Show Must Go On'

Column 1974 (singles):

Sweet, 'Teenage Rampage'
Mud, 'Tiger Feet'
Alice Cooper, 'Teenage Lament 74'
Lulu, 'The Man Who Sold the World'
T. Rex, 'Teenage Dream'
Alvin Stardust, 'Jealous Mind'
David Bowie, 'Rebel Rebel'
Glitter Band, 'Angel Face'
Mott the Hoople, 'The Golden Age of Rock 'n' Roll'
Sparks, 'This Town Ain't Big Enough for Both of Us'
Alvin Stardust, 'Red Dress'
Rubettes, 'Sugar Baby Love'
David Essex, 'America'
Cockney Rebel, 'Judy Teen'
Showaddywaddy, 'Hey Rock 'n' Roll'
Arrows, 'A Touch too Much'
Mott the Hoople, 'Foxy Foxy'
Sensational Alex Harvey Band, 'Sergeant Fury'
Sweet, 'The Six Teens'
Sparks, 'Amateur Hour'
Rolling Stones, 'It's Only Rock and Roll'
Cockney Rebel, 'Mr Soft'
Dana Gillespie, 'Andy Warhol'
David Bowie, 'Knock On Wood'
Roxy Music, 'All I Want Is You'
Slade, 'Far Far Away'
Sparks, 'Never Turn Your Back on Mother Earth'
Queen, 'Killer Queen'
Mott the Hoople, 'Saturday Gigs'
Hello, 'Tell Him'
Mud, 'Lonely this Christmas'
David Essex, 'Stardust'

Column 1975 (singles):

Sparks, 'Something for the Girl with Everything'
Suzi Quatro, 'Your Mama Won't Like Me'
Steve Harley & Cockney Rebel, 'Make Me Smile'
Slade, 'How Does It Feel'
Fox, 'Only You Can'
David Bowie, 'Young Americans'
Sweet, 'Fox on the Run'
Ian Hunter, 'Once Bitten Twice Shy'
Fox, 'Imagine Me, Imagine You'
Slade, 'Thanks for the Memory'
Steve Harley & Cockney Rebel, 'Mr Raffles'
T. Rex, 'New York City'
Sparks, 'Get in the Swing'
Sensational Alex Harvey Band, 'Delilah'
David Bowie, 'Fame'
Chris Spedding, 'Motorbiking'
Sparks, 'Looks Looks Looks'
Roxy Music, 'Love Is the Drug'
Hello, 'New York Groove'
Queen, 'Bohemian Rhapsody'
Sensational Alex Harvey Band, 'Gamblin' Bar Room Blues'
David Bowie, 'Golden Years'
Sailor, 'Glass of Champagne'
Roxy Music, 'Both Ends Burning'

1973 1974 1975

1973 (albums):

Alice Cooper, *Billion Dollar Babies*
Iggy & the Stooges, *Raw Power*
Roxy Music, *For Your Pleasure*
T. Rex, *Tanx*
Silverhead, *Silverhead*
David Bowie, *Aladdin Sane*
Sensational Alex Harvey Band, *Next*
Dana Gillespie, *Weren't Born a Man*
Mott the Hoople, *Mott*
Sylvester, *Sylvester and the Hot Band*
Lou Reed, *Berlin*
New York Dolls, *New York Dolls*
David Bowie, *Pinups*
Bryan Ferry, *These Foolish Things*
Roxy Music, *Stranded*
Eno, *Here Come the Warm Jets*
Alice Cooper, *Muscle of Love*
Cockney Rebel, *The Human Menagerie*
Jobriath, *Jobriath*

1974 (albums):

Mott the Hoople, *The Hoople*
T. Rex, *Zinc Alloy and the Hidden Riders of Tomorrow*
Slade, *Old, New, Borrowed and Blue*
Mick Ronson, *Slaughter on 10th Avenue*
Lou Reed, *Sally Can't Dance*
Kiss, *Kiss*
New York Dolls, *Too Much Too Soon*
David Bowie, *Diamond Dogs*
Slapp Happy, *Slapp Happy*
Silverhead, *Sixteen and Savaged*
Jobriath, *Creatures of the Street*
Sparks, *Kimono My House*
Cockney Rebel, *The Psychomodo*
Bryan Ferry, *Another Time Another Place*
Sailor, *Sailor*
Space Waltz, *Space Waltz*
Sensational Alex Harvey Band, *The Impossible Dream*
Roxy Music, *Country Life*
Eno, *Taking Tiger Mountain (by Strategy)*
Slade, *Flame*
Sparks, *Propaganda*

1975 (albums):

Mick Ronson, Play, *Don't Worry*
T. Rex, *Bolan's Zip Gun*
John Lennon, *Rock 'n' Roll*
Alice Cooper, *Welcome to My Nightmare*
David Bowie, *Young Americans*
Steve Harley & Cockney Rebel, *The Best Years of Our Lives*
Sensational Alex Harvey Band, *Tomorrow Belongs to Me*
Ian Hunter, *Ian Hunter*
Slapp Happy, *Desperate Straights*
Lou Reed, *Metal Machine Music*
Eno, *Another Green World*
Roxy Music, *Siren*
Sparks, *Indiscreet*
Sailor, *Trouble*

1973 (films/events):

American Graffiti (film)
That'll Be the Day (film)
The Rocky Horror Show (London stage)
Grease (London stage)
First independent radio stations in Britain
Big Biba opens (shop)

1974 (films/events):

Mahler (film)
Remember Me this Way (film)
Death Wish (film)
That's Entertainment! (film)
Phantom of the Paradise (film)
The Rocky Horror Show (first American production)
Happy Days (US television)
Technicians' strike blacks out *Top of the Pops*

1975 (films/events):

Flame (film)
Tommy (film)
The Rocky Horror Picture Show (film)
Lisztomania (film)
Never Too Young to Rock (film)
Teeth 'n' Smiles (London stage)
The Naked Civil Servant (television)
Cracked Actor (television)
Supersonic starts on television
Closure of Biba

1973 (news):

UK joins European Community
America ends involvement in Vietnam
School-leaving age raised from fifteen to sixteen in Britain
Yom Kippur War sparks oil crisis

1974 (news):

Three-day working week
Election (and then re-election) of Harold Wilson as prime minister
Patty Hearst kidnapped by the Symbionese Liberation Army
Watergate scandal leads to Richard Nixon resigning as US president

1975 (news):

Unemployment reaches 1 million
Inflation hits post-war peak of 26.9 per cent

REFERENCES

Note: Material derived from personal communication or correspondence is indicated thus: (pc).

INTRODUCTION:
FAR BEYOND THE PALE HORIZON

1 *NME*, 21 December 1974
2 *NME*, 7 December 1974
3 Dave Hill (pc)
4 Bruce 1996, p.87
5 *Mojo*, no.60, November 1998
6 Georg Kajanus (pc)
7 Andy Scott (pc)
8 Suzi Quatro (pc)
9 Lazell & Rees 1982, p.68
10 *Nashua Telegraph*, 4 November 1972
11 Hoskyns 1998, p.52
12 Nicky Chinn & Mike Chapman, 'Teenage Rampage' (BMG Music, 1974)
13 *Record Mirror*, 18 August 1973
14 *Guardian*, 9 October 1972
15 *Melody Maker*, 19 January 1974
16 Ray Davies, 'Celluloid Heroes' (Davray/Carlin, 1972)
17 Smith 1990, p.358
18 Strange 2002, p.40
19 *Nationwide* feature on David Bowie (broadcast May 1973)
20 David Bowie, 'Rebel, Rebel' (MainMan/Chrysalis Music, 1974)
21 *Sun*, 18 January 1974
22 McNeill & McCain 1997, p.4
23 *Melody Maker*, 26 January 1974
24 Clayson 1995, p.141
25 *Gay News*, July 1972
26 *Melody Maker*, 5 September 1970
27 Newell 2001, p.145
28 Green 1978, p.125
29 *Guardian*, 30 July 1953
30 Melly 1970, p.176
31 Bryan Ferry, 'A Really Good Time' (EG Music, 1974)
32 Hunter 1974, p.100
33 Dave Hill (pc)
34 Hoskyns 1998, p.58
35 Weird & Gilly 2003, p.86
36 Interview on DVD of *The Man Who Fell to Earth* (Anchor Bay, 2003)
37 Dave Hill (pc)
38 Doggett 2012, p.103
39 Marc Bolan, 'Get It On' (Essex Music, 1971)
40 David Bowie, 'Rock 'n' Roll Suicide' (MainMan/Chrysalis Music, 1972)
41 Eno, 'The Paw Paw Negro Blowtorch' (BMG Songs, 1973)
42 Michael Des Barres (pc)
43 Tinkler, *Marc Bolan* (BBC TV)
44 Lazell & Rees 1982, p.42
45 *Times*, 10 January 1973
46 Thomson & Gutman 1993, p.37
47 Bracewell 2007, p.358
48 Fisher 1973, pp.83–94
49 *Time* magazine, 30 October 1972
50 *Observer*, 19 November 1972
51 Bruce 1996, p.42
52 Lazell & Rees 1982, p.15

WHEN YOU ROCK AND ROLL WITH ME

1 Hastings/Toplady, 'Rock of Ages' (Carlin Music, 1973)
2 Andrew Matheson (pc)
3 Green 1978, p.71
4 Everett 1986, p.27
5 Rock & Bowie 2005, p.11
6 Frame 2007, p.433

1
A TALL HAT AND A TATTOOED GOWN

1 *Guardian*, 8 September 1973
2 McNeill & McCain 1997, p.54
3 Sandford 1997, p.74
4 David Bowie, 'Star' (MainMan/Chrysalis Music, 1972)
5 David Bowie, 'All the Young Dudes' (MainMan/Chrysalis Music, 1972)
6 Lazell & Rees 1982, p.63
7 *NME*, 27 March 1971
8 Bryan Ferry, 'Do the Strand' (EG Music, 1973)
9 David Bowie, 'Starman' (MainMan/Chrysalis Music, 1972)
10 *Guardian*, 24 January 1972
11 *Record Mirror*, 5 June 1971
12 *NME*, 18 December 1971
13 Newell 2001, p.211
14 Rogan 1982, p.38
15 *Guardian*, 4 November 1971
16 McNeill & McCain 1997, p.21
17 Green 1978, p.27
18 *Mojo*, no.28, March 1996
19 *Observer*, 29 January 1967
20 *Guardian*, 12 April 1971
21 *Melody Maker*, 6 July 1974
22 *Mojo*, no.104, July 2002
23 David Bowie, 'Little Toy Soldier' (copyright control, 1967)
24 Strange 2002, p.13
25 *Melody Maker*, 8 June 1974
26 Steve Harley, 'Death Trip' (RAK/Trigram Music, 1973)

27 David Bowie, 'Song for Bob Dylan' (MainMan/Chrysalis Music, 1971)
28 Devine 1998, p.86
29 Mick Ralphs, 'Rock and Roll Queen' (Blue Mountain Music, 1969)
30 *NME*, 13 February 1971
31 Devine 1998, p.93
32 *NME*, 4 December 1971
33 Holder 2000, p.81
34 *NME*, 17 July 1971
35 Mungham & Pearson 1976, p.110
36 *Times*, 10 January 1973
37 Cann 1983, p.73
38 Devine 1998, p.91
39 Bruce 1996, p.33
40 *Mojo*, no.145, December 2005
41 Bruce 1996, p.73
42 *Melody Maker*, 16 March 1974
43 Sharpe 2005, p.92
44 Rock & Bowie 2005, p.76
45 Trevor Bolder (pc)
46 *Melody Maker*, 12 January 1974
47 *Time* magazine, 30 October 1972
48 Green 1978, p.98
49 Cooper/Bruce/Buxton/Dunaway/Smith, 'Eighteen' (Bizarre Music/Ezra Music, 1970)
50 Marten & Hudson 2001, p.106
51 Ray Davies, 'Lola' (Davray/Carlin, 1971)
52 *Rolling Stone*, 9 November 1972
53 Ray Dorset (pc)
54 Visconti 2007, p.157
55 *Melody Maker*, 17 October 1970

HOLLYWOOD HIGHS

1 Sears/McDonald, 'Bogart to Bowie' (Black Dragon Music, 1974)
2 Hoskyns 1998, p.22
3 Hodkinson 1995, p.184
4 David Bowie, 'Life on Mars' (MainMan/Chrysalis Music, 1972)

2
GET DOWN AND GET WITH IT

1 *Record Mirror*, 23 January 1971
2 Oldham 2001, p.220
3 Green 1978, p.269
4 Connolly 1983, p.190
5 *Melody Maker*, 26 January 1974
6 *NME*, 13 November 1971
7 *Melody Maker*, 6 July 1974
8 *Times*, 29 November 1973
9 *NME*, 16 January 1971
10 Napier-Bell 1982, p.49
11 Oldham 2001, p.204
12 Tinkler, *Marc Bolan* (BBC TV)
13 *Times*, 14 January 1969
14 Visconti 2007, p.140
15 *NME*, 11 December 1971
16 *Record Mirror*, 17 April 1971
17 Hoskyns 1998, p.52
18 Antonia 2005, p.26
19 *Mojo*, no.47, October 1997
20 Visconti 2007, p.186
21 *Melody Maker*, 26 January 1974
22 Gambaccini 1975, p.27
23 Marc Bolan, 'Telegram Sam' (Wizard Publishing, 1972)
24 Marc Bolan, 'Children of the Revolution' (Wizard Publishing, 1972)
25 Marc Bolan, 'Metal Guru' (Wizard Publishing, 1972)
26 Marc Bolan, 'Ballrooms of Mars' (Wizard Publishing, 1972)
27 Marc Bolan, 'Rip-Off' (Essex Music, 1971)
28 *Mojo*, no.156, November 2006
29 Dave Hill (pc)
30 Holder 2000, p.125
31 *Mojo*, no.156, November 2006
32 Dave Hill (pc)
33 *Times*, 29 February 1972
34 Holder 2000, pp.121–2
35 *Mojo*, no.104, July 2002
36 David Bowie, 'Suffragette City' (MainMan/Chrysalis Music, 1972)
37 *Sunday Times*, 5 April 2009
38 Thatcher 1995, p.218
39 *Guardian*, 27 June 1972
40 *Times*, 14 September 1974
41 Benn 1989, p.247
42 *Times*, 12 October 1973
43 Isherwood 1978, p.53
44 *Life*, March 2004
45 David Bowie, 'Lady Stardust' (MainMan/Chrysalis Music, 1972)
46 Isherwood 1978, p.144
47 *Guardian*, 21 December 1972
48 Sherman 2009, p.56
49 Rogan 1982, p.38
50 *Guardian*, 15 April 1978
51 Gillman 1986, p.259
52 *NME*, 8 May 1971
53 McNeill & McCain 1997, p.155
54 Hoskyns 1998, pp.26–7
55 *NME*, 28 December 1974
56 Sandford 1997, p.82
57 Hoskyns 1998, p.28
58 Visconti 2007, p.147
59 Scott (ed.) 1972, p.5
60 Gillman 1986, p.272

THE BALLROOMS OF MARS

1 *NME*, 7 December 1974
2 *Time* magazine, 26 February 1973
3 *Time* magazine, 30 December 1957
4 Interview on DVD of *The Man Who Fell to Earth* (Anchor Bay, 2003)

3
I COULD MAKE A WILD MUTATION

1 *Mojo*, no.84, November 2000
2 Eager 2007, pp.170–1
3 *Mojo*, no.84, November 2000
4 Glitter 1992, p.20
5 Hunter 1974, p.8
6 *Melody Maker*, 30 March 1974
7 Connolly 1974, pp.136–7
8 *Times*, 2 September 1972
9 David Bowie, 'Moonage Daydream' (MainMan/Chrysalis Music, 1972)
10 David Bowie, 'Starman' (MainMan/Chrysalis Music, 1972)
11 David Bowie, 'Suffragette City' (MainMan/Chrysalis Music, 1972)
12 David Bowie, 'Ziggy Stardust' (MainMan/Chrysalis Music, 1972)
13 *Times*, 24 January 1973

14 David Bowie, 'Time' (MainMan/ Chrysalis Music, 1973)
15 *Times*, 9 December 1972
16 Hoskyns 2003, p.20
17 *Daily Telegraph*, 31 August 2002
18 David Bowie, 'Rock 'n' Roll Suicide' (MainMan/Chrysalis Music, 1972)
19 Burke 1967, p.142
20 *Time* magazine, 1 January 1973
21 Ellis 1964, p.80
22 *Sunday Times Magazine*, 4 November 2012
23 *Times*, 29 November 1973
24 *Melody Maker*, 26 January 1974
25 Glitter 1992, pp.91–2
26 *NME*, 27 March 1971
27 Bryan Ferry, 'If There Is Something' (E.G. Music, 1972)
28 Lazell & Rees 1982, p.8
29 Ferry/Manzanera, 'Out of the Blue' (E.G. Music, 1974)
30 Rogan 1982, p.79
31 *Guardian*, 9 October 1972
32 ibid.
33 *Mojo*, no.25, December 1995
34 David Bowie, 'Sweet Thing' (MainMan/Chrysalis Music, 1974)
35 Glitter 1992, p.103
36 Hoskyns 1998, p.22
37 Bracewell 2007, p.379
38 Lazell & Rees 1982, p.40
39 Rock & Bowie 2005, p.81
40 Hoskyns 1998, p.57
41 Cann 1983, p.95
42 Gillman 1986, p.294
43 Johnnie Walker, *The Autobiography* (London, 2008), p. 152
44 Herbie Flowers (pc)
45 *Record Mirror*, 8 September 1973
46 *Mojo*, no.60, November 1998
47 *Uncut*, no.128, January 2008
48 *Mojo*, no.60, November 1998
49 Devine 1998, p.150
50 *Times*, 2 July 1973
51 Paytress 2003, p.246
52 *Nashua Telegraph*, 4 November 1972
53 Devine 1998, p.141
54 *Observer*, 19 November 1972
55 *Melody Maker*, 9 March 1974

SOME KINDA TEMPORARY

1 McNeill & McCain 1997, p.159
2 ibid., p.148
3 Hunter 1974, p.52
4 Russell Mael (pc)
5 Bracewell 2007, p.365
6 *New Yorker*, 14 October 1972
7 Hunter 1974, p.9
8 Yentob, *Cracked Actor* (BBC TV)
9 Michael Des Barres (pc)
10 Lazell & Rees 1982, p.14
11 Rogan 1982, p.49
12 Lazell & Rees 1982, p.50
13 *Melody Maker*, 18 May 1974
14 Phil Pickett (pc)
15 Georg Kajanus (pc)
16 Sleeve-notes to Sylvester and the Hot Band, *The Blue Thumb*

Collection (Geffen Records, 2009)
17 Verden Allen/Ian Hunter, 'Hymn for the Dudes' (April Music/H&H Music, 1973)
18 Juby 1986, p.68
19 *Los Angeles Times*, 23 May 2009
20 Radice 2003, p.253
21 Drabble 1977, p.70
22 Balham 1977, p.105
23 Rogan 1982, p.57

24 Bryan Ferry/Andy Mackay, 'A Song for Europe' (E.G. Music, 1973)
25 Hoskyns 1998, p.57
26 *Melody Maker*, 10 August 1974
27 *Melody Maker*, 13 July 1974
28 *Record Mirror*, 3 August 1974
29 *Daily Express*, 14 May 1973
30 Rock & Bowie 2005, pp.189 and 215
31 Cann 1983, p.114
32 *Mojo*, no.47, October 1997
33 Devine 1998, p.181
34 Scott (ed.) 1974, p.93
35 *Record Mirror*, 4 August 1973
36 *Melody Maker*, 23 February 1974
37 Brian Eno, 'Some of Them Are Old' (BMG Songs, 1973)
38 Rogan 1982, p.130
39 *Melody Maker*, 12 January 1974
40 Hoskyns 1998, p.90
41 *Melody Maker*, 12 January 1974
42 *Mojo*, no.60, November 1998
43 Jobriath Boone, 'Blow Away' (Pierrot Music, 1973)
44 T. Roth, 'Little Boys' (copyright control, 1973)
45 Green 1978, p.15
46 *Record Mirror*, 1 December 1973
47 Mick Rock (pc)
48 Adam Ant (pc)
49 *Guardian*, 26 November 1973
50 *Daily Express*, 10 December 1973
51 *Record Mirror*, 27 October 1973
52 *Daily Express*, 5 October 1973

BIBA-NOVA

1 *Vogue*, 15 September 1973
2 *Observer*, 20 July 1975
3 *Mirabelle*, 6 October 1973
4 *Circus*, April 1975
5 *The Architect & Building News*, 14 April 1933
6 *Melody Maker*, 26 January 1974
7 *Melody Maker*, 11 October 1975

HEARTBEAT, INCREASING HEARTBEAT

1 *Guardian*, 4 February 1974
2 Bruce 1996, p.126
3 *Sunday Times*, 20 January 1974
4 *Mojo*, no.156, November 2006
5 Holder 2000, p.190

6 *Melody Maker*, 26 January 1974
7 *Melody Maker*, 26 January 1974
8 *Melody Maker*, 5 January 1974
9 Ian Hunter, 'Pearl 'n' Roy (England)' (April Music Inc/H&H Music, 1974)
10 Healey 1990, p.392
11 Devine 1998, p.199
12 *NME*, 19 October 1974
13 *NME*, 28 August 1971
14 Russell Mael (pc)
15 *Melody Maker*, 6 July 1974
16 *Melody Maker*, 29 June 1974
17 *Life*, March 2004
18 Scott (ed.) 1974, p.92
19 *Melody Maker*, 8 June 1974
20 *NME*, 2 November 1974
21 *Melody Maker*, 8 June 1974
22 Georg Kajanus (pc)
23 Phil Pickett (pc)
24 *Melody Maker*, 5 January 1974
25 David Courtney (pc)
26 *Music Week*, 3 April 2010
27 Tremlett 1976, p.85
28 Eager 2007, p.139
29 *Melody Maker*, 23 March 1974
30 Jeff Wayne (pc)
31 Herbie Flowers (pc)
32 Newell 2001, pp.190–1
33 *Mojo*, no.47, October 1997
34 Holder 2000, p.176
35 Everett 1986, p.124
36 Lorraine Kelly (pc)
37 *Mojo*, no.170, January 2008
38 Juby 1986, p.59
39 *Daily Mirror*, 8 January 1972
40 *Melody Maker*, 18 May 1974
41 *Record Mirror*, 11 August 1973
42 George 1995, p.36
43 David Bowie, 'The Bewlay Brothers' (MainMan/Chrysalis Music, 1971)
44 David Bowie, 'Sweet Thing' (MainMan/Chrysalis Music, 1974)
45 David Bowie, 'Lady Stardust' (MainMan/Chrysalis Music, 1972)
46 *Uncut*, no.128, January 2008
47 *Record Mirror*, 21 July 1973
48 *Melody Maker*, 18 May 1974
49 *Record Mirror*, 6 July 1974
50 Lulu 2002, p.172
51 Suzi Quatro (pc)
52 *Melody Maker*, 2 March 1974
53 *Record Mirror*, 4 August 1973
54 *Melody Maker*, 16 February 1974
55 Suzi Quatro (pc)
56 Rob Davis (pc)
57 Andy Scott (pc)
58 *Melody Maker*, 9 February 1974
59 Mike Chapman/Nicky Chinn, 'Teenage Rampage' (BMG Music Publishing, 1974)
60 *Melody Maker*, 12 January 1974
61 Mike Chapman/Nicky Chinn, 'Turn It Down' (BMG Music Publishing, 1974)
62 *Record Mirror*, 14 December 1974
63 Logan & Woffinden 1977, p.189
64 Hodkinson 1995, p.186
65 *NME*, 2 November 1974
66 Oscar Wilde, *Lady Windermere's Fan* Act III
67 Freddie Mercury, 'We Are the Champions' (B. Feldman/Trident Music, 1977)
68 Phil Wainman (pc)
69 Andy Scott (pc)

TUMBLING DOWN

1 *Melody Maker*, 12 January 1974
2 David Bowie, 'Future Legend' (MainMan/Chrysalis Music, 1974)
3 *Daily Mail*, 11 March 1975
4 *Sun*, 9 April 1975
5 *Sun*, 22 January 1977
6 David Bowie, 'Diamond Dogs' (MainMan/Chrysalis Music, 1974)
7 Sandford 1997, p.126
8 Juby 1986, p.77
9 *Guardian*, 24 October 1974
10 Weird and Gilly 2003, p.85
11 David Bowie, 'Hang On to Yourself' (MainMan/Chrysalis Music, 1972)
12 Steve Harley, 'Tumbling Down' (Trigram/RAK Publishing, 1974)
13 *NME*, 2 November 1974
14 *Record Mirror*, 3 August 1974
15 *Record Mirror*, 24 August 1974
16 *NME*, 6 September 75
17 *NME*, 2 January 1974
18 *Melody Maker*, 7 September 1974
19 Hoskyns 1998, p.92
20 Sherman 2009, p.24
21 *Mojo*, no.156, November 2006
22 *NME*, 14 September 1974
GH *Melody Maker*, 12 October 1974
24 Rogan 1982, p.115
25 *Melody Maker*, 15 June 1974
26 Orwell 1954, p.59
27 *Melody Maker*, 21 September 1974
28 *Record Mirror*, 11 August 1973
29 *Melody Maker*, 16 February 1974
30 Chris Norman (pc)
31 Holder 2000, p.190
32 *Melody Maker*, 13 July 1974
33 *Sun*, 18 February 1977
34 Visconti 2007, p.189
35 *Mojo*, no.156, November 2006
36 John Springate (pc)
37 *NME*, 14 September 1974
38 *NME*, 12 October 1974
39 Grant Gillanders, sleeve-notes to Alastair Riddell, *Space Waltz* (RPM Records, 2005)
40 *Melody Maker*, 2 March 1974
41 *Mojo*, no.47, October 1997
42 Devine 1998, p.248
43 Ian Hunter, 'Saturday Gigs' (April Music Inc/H&H Music, 1974)
44 Dave Hill (pc)
45 *Record Mirror*, 14 September 1974
46 Strange 2002, p.69
47 Archive material in booklet for CD reissue (Ozit Records, 1998)
48 Kid Strange, 'Mainlines' (Lupus Music, 1976)
49 *NME*, November 1973
50 *Record Mirror*, 3 August 1974
51 John Springate (pc)
52 Dave Hill (pc)
53 Visconti 2007, p.120
54 Phil Wainman (pc)

AFTER ALL
1 Trevor Bolder (pc)

BIBLIOGRAPHY

Note: Where a paperback or revised edition is shown, it indicates that any page references in the text are to that edition.

Nina Antonia, *Too Much, Too Soon: The Make-Up and Break-Up of the New York Dolls* (London, 1998)

Nina Antonia, *The Prettiest Star: Whatever Happened to Brett Smiley* (London, 2005)

Joe Balham, *The Sweeney: Regan and the Bent Stripper* (London, 1977)

Tony Benn (ed. Ruth Winstone), *Office Without Power: Diaries 1968–72* (London, 1988; pbk edn: 1989)

Peter Biskind, *Easy Riders, Raging Bulls* (London, 1998)

Michael Bracewell, *Remake/Remodel: Art, Pop, Fashion and the Making of Roxy Music, 1953–1972* (London, 2007)

Michael Bruce with Billy James, *No More Mr Nice Guy: The Inside Story of the Alice Cooper Group* (London, 1996)

David Buckley, *Strange Fascination: David Bowie – The Definitive Story* (London, 1999; revised pbk edn: 2005)

John Burke, *Privilege* (London, 1967)

Kevin Cann, *David Bowie: A Chronology* (London, 1983)

Philip Cato, *Crash Course for the Ravers: A Glam Odyssey* (Lockerbie, 1997)

Alan Clayson, *The Beat Merchants: The Origins, History, Impact and Rock Legacy of the 1960s British Pop Groups* (London, 1995)

Ray Connolly, *Stardust* (London, 1974)

Ray Connolly, *Stardust Memories: Talking about My Generation* (London, 1983)

Campbell Devine, *All the Young Dudes: Mott the Hoople and Ian Hunter – The Official Biography* (London, 1998)

Peter Doggett, *The Man Who Sold the World: David Bowie and the 1970s* (London, 2011; pbk edn: 2012)

Margaret Drabble, *The Ice Age* (London, 1977)

Vince Eager, *Rock 'n' Roll Files* (Radcliffe on Trent, 2007)

Royston Ellis, *Myself for Fame* (London, 1964)

Peter Everett, *You'll Never Be 16 Again: An Illustrated History of the British Teenager* (London, 1986)

John Fisher, *Funny Way to Be a Hero* (London, 1973)

Pete Frame, *The Restless Generation: How Rock Music Changed the Face of 1950s Britain* (London, 2007)

Paul Gambaccini (ed.), *Elton John and Bernie Taupin* (London, 1975)

Paul Gambaccini, Tim Rice and Jonathan Rice, *British Hit Albums* (London, 1983; fifth edn: 1992)

Boy George, *Take It Like a Man* (London, 1995; pbk edn: 1995)

Peter and Leni Gillman, *Alias David Bowie: A Biography* (Sevenoaks, 1986)

Gary Glitter with Lloyd Bradley, *Leader: The Autobiography* (London, 1991; pbk edn: 1992)

Jonathon Green (ed.), *The Book of Rock Quotes* (London, 1977; rev. edn: 1978)

Jonathon Green, *Days in the Life: Voices from the English Underground 1961–1971* (London, 1988; pbk edn: 1998)

Denis Healey, *The Time of My Life* (London, 1989; pbk edn: 1990)

Mark Hodkinson, *Queen: the Early Years* (London, 1995)

Noddy Holder with Lisa Verrico, *Who's Crazee Now? My Autobiography* (London, 1999; rev. pbk edn: 2000)

Barney Hoskyns, *Glam! Bowie, Bolan and the Glitter Rock Revolution* (London, 1998)

Barney Hoskyns (ed.), *The Sound and the Fury: A Rock's Backpages Reader – 40 Years of Classic Rock Journalism* (London, 2003)

Ian Hunter, *Diary of a Rock 'n' Roll Star* (St Albans, 1974)

Christopher Isherwood, *Christopher and His Kind* (London, 1977; pbk edn: 1978)

Tony Jasper (ed.), *British Record Charts 1955–1979* (London, 1979)

Kerry Juby, *In Other Words … David Bowie* (London, 1986)

Barry Lazell and Dafydd Rees, *Bryan Ferry and Roxy Music* (London, 1982)

Nick Logan and Bob Woffinden (ed.), *The Illustrated New Musical Express Encyclopedia of Rock* (London, 1977)

Lulu, *I Don't Want to Fight* (London, 2002)

Legs McNeil and Gillian McCain, *Please Kill Me: The Uncensored Oral History of Punk* (London, 1996; pbk edn: London, 1997)

Neville Marten and Jeff Hudson, *Well Respected Men* (revised edn: London, 2001; orig. pub. as *The Kinks*, Chessington, 1996)

George Melly, *Revolt into Style: The Pop Arts in Britain* (London, 1970)

Geoff Mungham and Geoff Pearson, *Working-Class Youth Culture* (London, 1976)

Simon Napier-Bell, *You Don't Have to Say You Love Me* (London, 1982)

Martin Newell, *This Little Ziggy* (Wivenhoe, 2001)

Andrew Loog Oldham, *Stoned* (London, 2000; pbk edn: 2001)

George Orwell, *Nineteen Eighty-Four*
(London, 1949; pbk edn: Harmondsworth, 1954)

Mark Paytress, *The Rolling Stones
off the Record: Outrageous Opinions
and Unrehearsed Interviews*
(London, 2003)

Giles Radice, *Friends and Rivals:
Crosland, Jenkins and Healey*
(London, 2002; pbk edn: 2003)

David Roberts (ed.), *The Guinness
Book of British Hit Singles*
(1977 – 14th edition: London, 2001)

Mick Rock and David Bowie,
*Moonage Daydream: The Life and
Times of Ziggy Stardust*
(London, 2005; orig. pub. Guildford, 2002)

Johnny Rogan, *Roxy Music:
Style with Substance – Roxy's First Ten Years*
(London, 1982)

Christopher Sandford, *Bowie:
Loving the Alien*
(London, 1996; rev. pbk edn: 1997)

Jack Scott (ed.), *New Musical Express
1973 Annual*
(London, 1972)

Jack Scott (ed.), *New Musical Express
Greatest Hits: The Very Best of NME*
(London, 1974)

Graham Sharpe, *The Man Who Was
Screaming Lord Sutch*
(London, 2005)

Dale Sherman, *Black Diamond: The Unauthorized
Biography of Kiss*
(London, 2009)

Joe Smith (ed. Mitchell Fink), *Off the Record:
An Oral History of Popular Music*
(London, 1989; pbk edn: 1990)

Cathi Stein, *Elton John*
(London, 1975)

Richard Strange, *Strange:
Punks and Drunks and Flicks and Kicks
– the Memoirs of Richard Strange*
(London, 2002)

Margaret Thatcher, *The Path to Power*
(London, 1995)

Elizabeth Thomson and David Gutman (eds),
The Bowie Companion
(London, 1993)

George Tremlett, *The Alvin Stardust Story*
(London, 1976)

Alwyn W. Turner, *Crisis? What Crisis?
Britain in the 1970s*
(London, 2008)

Tony Visconti, *The Autobiography: Bowie,
Bolan and the Brooklyn Boy*
(London, 2007)

Weird and Gilly, *Mick Ronson: The Spider
with the Platinum Hair*
(London, 2003)

Joel Whitburn, *The Billboard Book of USA
Top 40 Albums*
(Enfield, 1987)

Joel Whitburn, *The Billboard Book of USA
Top 40 Hits*
(Enfield, 1989)

FILMS AND TELEVISION

Note: This list is restricted to those works that are quoted in the text.

Bonnie and Clyde – dir: Arthur Penn,
wr: David Newman and Robert Benton
(Warner Brothers/Seven Arts, 1967)

Cracked Actor – dir: Alan Yentob
(BBC Television, 1975)

Marc Bolan: The Final Word – dir: Mark Tinkler
(Double Jab Productions for BBC Television, 2007)

The Naked Civil Servant – dir: Jack Gold,
wr: Philip Mackie
(Thames TV, 1975)

Privilege – dir: Peter Watkins,
wr: Norman Bogner
(Universal Pictures, 1966)

The Sheik – dir: George Melford,
wr: Monte M. Katterjohn
(Paramount Pictures, 1921)

Stardust – dir: Michael Apted,
wr: Ray Connolly
(EMI Films, 1974)

PICTURE CREDITS

Unless otherwise specified, images are © Victoria and Albert Museum, London

ACKNOWLEDGEMENTS

My thanks are primarily due to those who've been kind enough to speak with me and share their memories and thoughts about glam, as well as those who have helped with various queries. These include: Adam Ant, Alan Williams, Andrew Matheson, Andy Scott, Chris Norman, Chris Spedding, Dave Bartram, Dave Courtney, Dave Hill, David Blaylock, David Foster-Smith, Eddie Seago, Georg Kajanus, Herbie Flowers, Jeff Wayne, John Rossall, John Springate, Jonathan King, Karl Stoeker, Kevin Smith, Lorraine Kelly, Michael Des Barres, Michelle Coomber, Mick Rock, Mike Sweeney, Milton Reame-James, Nina Antonia, Paul Thomas, Phil Pickett, Phil Wainman, Pip Williams, Ray Dorset, Ray Stiles, Rob Davies, Roger Crimlis, Russell Mael, Steve Jones, Steve Thomas, Suzi Quatro, Trevor Bolder, Vince Eager and Wayne Bickerton. I'm also grateful to those who didn't wish to be named or quoted directly.

Thanks too to everyone at the V&A, including Davina Cheung, Clare Davis, Geoffrey Marsh, Kate Bailey, Kate Phillimore, Rachel Malig, Richard Davis, Will Webb, and particularly to Frances Ambler, who's been a fine editor, and, as ever, to Mark Eastment.

Chapter titles are taken from the following songs: Roxy Music, 'Virginia Plain'; T. Rex, 'Ride a White Swan'; Slade, 'Get Down and Get With It'; David Bowie, 'Star'; Mott the Hoople, 'Hymn for the Dudes'; Sparks, 'This Town Ain't Big Enough for Both of Us'; Cockney Rebel, 'Tumbling Down'.

Titles for the picture-spreads are taken from 'When You Rock and Roll With Me', 'Cracked Actor' and 'After All' by David Bowie, and 'The Ballrooms of Mars' and 'Spaceball Richochet' by T. Rex, as well as 'Biba-Nova' (from the TV series *Rock Follies*) and 'Science Fiction/Double Feature' from *The Rocky Horror Show*.

This book is dedicated to John Flaxman,
who does like a bit of glam.

INDEX

Page numbers in italic refer to the captions